AF579254

40 LOVE STORIES THAT INSPIRED OUR FAVORITE FILMS

KRISTEN LOPEZ

ILLUSTRATED BY
JYOTIRMAYEE PATRA

RUNNING PRESS
PHILADELPHIA

Running Press
Hachette Book Group
1290 Avenue of the Americas, New York, NY 10104
www.runningpress.com
@Running_Press

First Edition: July 2026

Published by Running Press, an imprint of Hachette Book Group, Inc.
The Running Press name and logo are trademarks of Hachette Book Group, Inc.

Print book cover and interior design by Amanda Richmond

Library of Congress Cataloging-in-Publication Data
Names: Lopez, Kristen author | Turner Classic Movies (Firm) other
Title: But have you read the book? romance edition : 40 love stories that inspired our favorite films / Kristen Lopez, Turner Classic Movies.
Description: First edition. | Philadelphia : Running Press, 2026. | Includes bibliographical references. | Summary: "For film buffs and literature lovers alike, Turner Classic Movies presents an essential guide to 40 cinema classics and the love stories that served as their inspiration" —Provided by publisher.
Identifiers: LCCN 2025034741 (print) | LCCN 2025034742 (ebook) | ISBN 9798894142296 hardcover | ISBN 9798894142302 ebook
Subjects: LCSH: Film adaptations—Encyclopedias | Romance films—Encyclopedias | Romance fiction—Encyclopedias | Motion pictures and literature | LCGFT: Film criticism | Literary criticism
Classification: LCC PN1997.85 .L675 2026 (print) | LCC PN1997.85 (ebook) | DDC 791.43/6—dc23/eng/20250811
LC record available at https://lccn.loc.gov/2025034741
LC ebook record available at https://lccn.loc.gov/2025034742

ISBNs: 979-8-89414-229-6 (hardcover), 979-8-89414-230-2 (ebook)

Printed in China

TLF

10 9 8 7 6 5 4 3 2 1

To my family.

Thank you for everything.

Contents

Introduction

SCARLETT O'HARA AND RHETT BUTLER. ELIZABETH Bennett and Mr. Darcy. You can't think of one without the other. When the stars align, the perfect literary couple transcends the pages of their story to become an iconic pop culture duo. In 1740, author Samuel Richardson wrote what is commonly considered the first romance novel: *Pamela; or, Virtue Rewarded*. It's an epistolary novel—told through letters—about a naive maidservant and her struggle to resist the advances of her employer. The success of Richardson's novel brought a host of imitators and crafted a genre that has continued to make readers swoon, and set high expectations for a paramour, for centuries. Since that time, we've seen romance manifest in gloomy landscapes, like the dark halls of Anya Seton's *Dragonwyck*. We've gone from the sands of the Middle East in *The Sheik* to contemporary Jamaica in *How Stella Got Her Groove Back*.

The best couples in a literary romance are able to overcome their differences and support each other. In Erich Segal's *Love Story*, couple Jenny and Oliver deal with having different socioeconomic backgrounds and religions. But when Jenny becomes ill, Oliver is a source of strength and comfort. Con man and bank robber Jack Foley and US marshal Karen Sisco are on opposite ends of the law in *Out of Sight*, but thrill at the cat-and-mouse nature of their relationship. Rhett Butler helps Scarlett O'Hara survive the Civil War in *Gone with the Wind* in spite of Scarlett's selfishness and love for another man. And in Nicholas Sparks's *The Notebook*, everyman Noah builds a house and reads a nightly story to his beloved Allie. These characters show us what true love looks like. These relationships may be an unattainable ideal, but they help us understand what we're willing to accept (or not) in a relationship. Much like Old Hollywood, we consume the fantasy and wrap ourselves up in escapism.

But romance is a genre that is a time capsule of its era, and as gender roles and modern understandings of domestic violence and assault come into play, readers are required to look at some books with an awareness of the time the author lived in, compelling modern-day readers to question their usage in the book while still engaging with the relationships at the center.

Romance novels can also show dated depictions of what's considered feminine. Books like *Waiting to Exhale* and *Bridget Jones's Diary* hyperfocus on women's weight, representative of their 1990s setting, while *Jane Eyre* shows its title heroine enduring all manner of suffering only to be rewarded with a husband at the end. But for every book like that, there's another wherein the author subversively rails against the limitations placed on women. Author Vera Caspary's *Laura* is a noir love story that emphasizes how much autonomy women in the 1940s had through getting a job. Laura Hunt (Gene Tierney) in the novel enjoys working and only begrudgingly considers marriage. Robert Nathan's *The Bishop's Wife* is less a Christmas romance compared to its 1947 Cary Grant–starring feature and more about religious devotion. Julia (Loretta Young) seeks physical affection from her minister husband and feels bad about it. And R. A. Dick's *The Ghost and Mrs. Muir* might shock lovers of the 1947 novel, as there's just enough ambiguity in there to make the reader question whether the seafaring ghost in the heroine's mind is less a romantic lead and more a manifestation of a repressed woman's conscience.

When the first volume of *But Have You Read the Book?* debuted in 2023 it covered several enduring romance novels, including *The Princess Bride*, *Wuthering Heights*, and *Call Me By Your Name*, so if you're asking, "Why isn't [insert romance book] in here?" be sure to give that one a read. My goal was to hit the biggest movies, and some of the biggest trends, of romance adaptation, such as the move away from employee/employer relationships and the different ways tragic romances are showcased. I tried not to repeat authors, with the exception of Terry McMillan—one of the essential Black female authors writing in the 1990s—and E. M. Forster, whose book *Maurice* is considered a groundbreaking work of LGTBQ+ fiction. There were also quite a few romance films I didn't include either because they were a tad too similar to other books on the list (like *Washington Square*), out of print, or I just plain forgot about them (sorry, *High Fidelity* and *The Scarlet Letter*). Regardless, there's plenty of love to be found within these pages and I hope *But Have You Read the Book? Romance Edition* makes you sigh, makes you smile, and doesn't break your heart.

Kristen Lopez

THE SHEIK

1921

Directed by George Melford
Screenplay by Monte M. Katterjohn
Based on *The Sheik* by Edith Maud Hull, 1919

"Diana, my beloved! The darkness has passed and now the sunshine."

A harsh, oppressive desert. A kidnapped woman searches for escape. A powerful, dominating sheik is desperate to possess her, body and soul. This sets the tone for E. M. Hull's 1919 novel *The Sheik*, an adventurous tale of romance in the Algerian desert. Lady Diana Mayo (Agnes Ayres) is a tomboyish woman of means desperate to go out on a desert adventure alone. She quickly catches the eye of Sheik Ahmed Ben Hassan (Rudolph Valentino), who kidnaps her with the intention of making her one of his mistresses. Diana is at first desperate to return to her staid English landscape, but soon discovers she is actually in love with the sheik. Will the couple be able to survive their class and racial differences, as well as the villainous rival Sheik Omair (Walter Long)?

The different incarnations of *The Sheik*, film and novel, are stark representations of their respective time periods, depicting romance and Middle Eastern culture in a way that is woefully out of date today. However, each illustrates how gender roles and ethnic stereotypes were depicted on-screen during the early twentieth century.

Author Edith Maud Hull turned to writing while her husband fought in World War I. *The Sheik*, her debut novel, was a smash hit and bestseller upon release, putting Hull on the map. Hull pulled from several popular literary traditions of the time for her novel, particularly the Orientalist genre, wherein white Western writers crafted their own fantasy depictions of the Middle East. Hull portrays Ahmed as a mysterious, frightening figure from the minute he kidnaps Diana, his aggression being a turn-on for her. Hull plays on the stereotype that Ahmed is an alluring—literally intoxicating—figure whose sexuality comes from being exotic and foreign. When he kisses her, Diana says, "it was like a narcotic, drugging [her] almost to insensibility." This Orientalist stereotyping also sees the poor, virginal Diana in the push-pull of being simultaneously drawn and repulsed by Ahmed's "savage" Arab ways, a fact not helped by his continual sexual assault of her starting the first night he abducts her. Sexual assault is also a common stereotype of romance literature in this era.

The 1921 film adaptation is a close translation of Hull's book, though where Hull plays on Orientalist stereotypes and romance novels' tropes of "ravaging" her female protagonist, the film is a straightforward romance in the tradition of silent-era adventure films. Italian actor Rudolph Valentino's performance as Sheik Ahmed Ben Hassan has become one of the most imitated and criticized depictions of an Arab character in cinema history, but the performance succeeded in making him an international star and sex symbol. Valentino conveys the sexual potency Hull writes of in the book, and the viewer witnesses his transformation from a man seeking control of Diana to wanting to earn her love and respect.

Thankfully, the film omits the multiple instances of rape Ahmed commits against Diana after her kidnapping. Film critics of the time actually complained about this change, saying it

altered the original message of Hull's book, but it's impossible to justify wanting the couple to get together otherwise. A *Variety* review published upon the release of the cinematic version of *The Sheik* explained why removing the assault undermined Hull's story as such: "The same novel, preposterous and ridiculous as it was, won out because it dealt with every caged woman's desire to be caught up in a love clasp by some he-man who would take responsibility and dispose of the consequences."

The idea of "rough wooing" isn't acceptable today, but at the time it was perceived as romantic; the Sheik being so in love with Diana that he must steal her. Critics have compared the "forced seduction" (i.e., rape) of Diana to the character dynamics in William Shakespeare's *Taming of the Shrew* and other romance novels of the day that sold the concept of a woman being "ravaged" or "taken" in a similar fashion.

In the book, Diana is completely unfeminine, brought up by a brother who doesn't know anything about women. Diana is raised like a boy, even wearing male clothes and having a short haircut. Because of her childhood, Diana bemoans her sex: "God made me a woman. Why, only He knows." For as much as Diana champions her independence, she also enjoys having her brother make all her decisions for her. Despite her independence, Diana truly wants a man to take charge and point her in a specific direction. Those who have championed Hull's work have said the author looks at the various questions feminists of the 1900s–1920s were actively discussing regarding female autonomy. As Hull said in an interview at the time, "I don't wish to . . . defend the callous brutality of Ahmed Ben Hassan . . . But I am old fashioned enough to believe that a woman's best love is given to the man . . . she recognizes is her master." The novel ends with Diana and Ahmed madly in love, which some critics have argued places Diana in a dominant position, so Ahmed falls in love with her *because* she is willing to challenge him. The fact that Ahmed and Diana end the book not only in love with each other but desiring to stay in the desert also breaks from typical romance traditions of the time period, wherein the presumption was that true safety and domesticity is exclusively found in European enclaves.

The book's ending owes its life to Edgar Rice Burroughs's *Tarzan* series, the first of which was released in 1912. Like that series, both versions of *The Sheik* end with the reveal that Ahmed is not a Middle Eastern man at all but is actually English. The book explores this reveal in more depth than the movie, as Ahmed's best friend Dr. Raoul de St. Hubert (Adolphe Menjou) documents the story of Ahmed's Spanish mother, who, while pregnant, fled into the desert to escape her drunk English husband. She is found by the elder Sheik Ahmed Ben

Hassan, who falls in love with her and, upon her death, raises her child as his own. Ahmed coming from English and Spanish stock is another era-specific romance trope and for film is doubly important: Due to anti-miscegenation laws in some states where the movie was shown, depicting two lovers of different ethnicities together at the end was forbidden. Ahmed is redeemed, both personally and spiritually, by garnering the love of a pure (white) woman, which further removes any perceived racial impurities between them.

In spite of how synonymous he became with the role, Valentino was not the original choice for *The Sheik*'s male lead. Producer Jesse Lasky wanted James Kirkwood in the part, but after hearing his secretary's enthusiastic endorsement for Valentino, coupled with the still-neophyte actor's low salary and ethnic appearance, Lasky changed course. Valentino himself tried to emphasize the falsity of the movie's depiction of Arabs at the time, saying in an interview that "[P]eople are not savages because they have dark skin." Five years later the studio released *The Son of the Sheik* (1926), an adaptation of Hull's follow-up book. Sadly, Valentino didn't live to see its release, dying of peritonitis at the age of thirty-one.

While the book and movie are dated for today's audiences, *The Sheik* is a fascinating example of romance during that period. Valentino's draw as a sex symbol shows what audiences of the time saw as the apotheosis of the dashing leading man. And the concept of the "other" remains a popular romance trope today, most prominently in monstrous romances like *Twilight* (2008), while the rough wooing conceit has softened and transformed into more of an "opposites attract" principle, or the "enemies to lovers" concept seen in teen dramas like *10 Things I Hate About You* (1999) and *Pride and Prejudice*.

ANNA KARENINA

1935

Directed by Clarence Brown
Screenplay by Clemence Dane and Salka Viertel
Based on *Anna Karenina* by Leo Tolstoy, 1878

"We'll be punished for being so happy."

Author Leo Tolstoy famously opens his novel *Anna Karenina* with the line, "All happy families are alike; each unhappy family is unhappy in its own way." *Anna Karenina* is a story about love, but it's also about how the union of two souls, and the subsequent community that flourishes from it, comes with its own set of problems, whether those be personal, political, or social. Since its publication in 1878 audiences have been enraptured by the story of the titular daring Russian beauty and her illicit romance with the enigmatic Count Vronsky. Tolstoy's book, clocking in at a whopping eight hundred pages (depending on the translation you're reading) is a vast exploration of everything from the interrelationship between passion and duty to the changing perception of Russia and its history, as well as the precarious position of women during the nineteenth century. With an expansive group of characters from various families, all with rich and complex interior lives, it's not surprising Hollywood sought to tell the story as succinctly as possible.

Anna Karenina was first adapted for American audiences in 1915 with Danish actress Betty Nansen as Anna. Sadly, little is known about this interpretation as the movie is considered lost with no known surviving prints existing. In 1927, MGM gave Swedish actress Greta Garbo her first opportunity to play the doomed Anna in *Love*, a silent film pairing her with on-screen (and off-screen) paramour John Gilbert as Vronksy. The film was a success and proved that audiences couldn't get enough of Garbo and Gilbert, despite the movie being 82 minutes and omitting much of Tolstoy's novel. (Some US audiences also saw an alternate happy ending rather than the more tragic one faithful to the book).

In 1935, the desire to adapt *Anna Karenina* as a talkie grew, though producer David O. Selznick wasn't too keen on Garbo, who was close to thirty, reprising the title character. He cited the failures of past costume pictures as well as disappointing returns on previous Garbo-led literary adaptations like *Queen Christina* (1933) and *The Painted Veil* (1934). Instead, he wanted her to do *Dark Victory*, a similarly tragic (albeit contemporary) love story, about a woman dying of a brain tumor, with director George Cukor. The finished film, released in 1939, netted star Bette Davis an Oscar nomination.

But Garbo was hell-bent on playing Anna Karenina, reuniting with director Clarence Brown for the sixth of their seven film collaborations. Fredric March played the valiant Vronsky, while Basil Rathbone—fresh off another literary adaptation, *David Copperfield* (1935)—plays Anna's straitlaced, vain husband, Karenin. (Unfortunately, Garbo and March did not get along while working on the film. March didn't want to do another costume picture, and Garbo, uninterested in being seduced by a ladies' man like March, was reported to wear garlic during their scenes together. Selznick also didn't want March in the role, offering it to Ronald Colman and Clark Gable first.)

The relationship between Vronsky and Anna is one of tragedy. They are doomed to love each other and doomed to be forever torn apart. Because of its brisk 95-minute run time, the movie emphasizes the affair between Anna and Vronsky before she eventually dies by suicide by jumping in front of a moving train. Societal forces that destroyed her relationship, coupled with her guilt about her son, Sergei (Freddie Bartholomew), lead to her suicide in the movie. But in the book, Tolstoy adds far more of the story.

Several of the book's subplots end up on the cutting room floor or are only hinted at, like the philandering ways of Anna's brother, Stiva (Reginald Owen), or the relationship between the independent-minded Levin (Gyles Isham) and the sweet Kitty (Maureen O'Sullivan). This latter plotline gets more weight in Tolstoy's novel than Anna and Vronsky's, as Levin struggles to find meaning and purpose in his life. He eventually realizes his deep love for Kitty and his children when their lives are threatened in a lightning storm. The novel also features a drawn-out backstory for Anna's husband, Karenin, who is portrayed as a cool-eyed villain in the movie. Tolstoy ties Vronsky and Karenin together in their mutual love of rules and rationality. Karenin and Anna also have more of a push-and-pull dynamic in the novel, with each deciding to divorce the other (or not) multiple times.

Anna Karenina is not autobiographical, but Tolstoy based much of the story on his life and interactions as a Russian citizen. Born into a large landowning family, Tolstoy lost his mother at the age of two. In the book, Anna's love for Vronsky is balanced with her deep love for her child, Sergei (called Seryozha), who is told his mother has died after she decides to live an adulterous life with Vronsky. Seryozha in the book goes from young child to teenager with little memory of his mother at all. It's theorized that Tolstoy based Seryozha on his own experiences growing up without a mother. Tolstoy went to Kazan University, where he studied law and Oriental languages and eventually married Sofia Andreevna, a relationship that served as the basis for Levin and Kitty.

The novel focuses on a married woman's affair, but Tolstoy's Anna is no femme fatale. When Vronsky first meets Anna, he takes notice of her gray eyes—a trait cited by Shakespeare in describing his female characters, as well as being the eye color of Athena, the goddess of wisdom. Much of their relationship on the page is about how they have more of a spiritual connection than a physical one. When the couple consummates their relationship, Anna cries and goes through a process of mourning because she understands this action is the point of no return. Since that couldn't be discussed on-screen due to the Hays Code, screenwriters Dane and Viertel make Anna torn between her love for Vronsky and her maternal instincts. Regardless, the Hays Code still had issues with the film depicting what they felt was an affair without consequences.

Garbo conveys the consequences of her relationship with Vronsky in her tortured glances and quiet smiles. It's a performance filled with a stoic bearing, unlike other portrayals of Anna Karenina that are more melodramatic. As Clarence Brown once said about Garbo, "She was a shy person; her lack of English gave her a slight inferiority complex. I used to direct her quietly. I never gave her direction above a whisper." In Garbo's hands the character is desperate for love, torn between her own personal quest for romance and her love for her son. Where is the line drawn between personal happiness and selfishness, between familial duty and personal autonomy? Tolstoy's Anna on the page understands she can't find a happy medium between the two; she must always choose. It's better to die than to let anyone down, including herself.

Garbo's Anna dies the death of a woman who gambled on love and lost. Her suicide in the movie plays as the result of her belief that Vronsky no longer loves her. She watches him flirt with another woman. The novel's Anna is more impulsive and commits suicide to "be rid of everybody," including herself, after the reader has spent countless pages watching her mentally corrode. She has a moment of regret right before the train arrives. But in both Garbo's and Tolstoy's conception of the character, Anna is an outsider who does everything for the love of something, whether it's a paramour, her son, or herself.

This adaptation wasn't the last time Anna's tragic story received the big-screen treatment. Vivien Leigh played the character in a 1948 interpretation directed by Julien Duvivier. Fans either consider Leigh or Garbo to be the definitive Anna Karenina. Leigh plays the character less like the fiercely independent Scarlett O'Hara in *Gone with the Wind*, who holds some commonalities with Tolstoy's written character, and more like Myra Lester, the doomed ballerina in Leigh's remake of *Waterloo Bridge* (1940). And in 2012, director Joe Wright reunited with his *Atonement* star Keira Knightley in the title role and Aaron Taylor-Johnson as Vronsky to tell the story again, this time with an expanded 130-minute run time to flesh out the Levin character (played by Domhnall Gleeson).

CAMILLE

1936

Directed by George Cukor
Screenplay by Zoe Akins, Frances Marion, and James Hilton
Based on *The Lady of the Camellias*
by Alexandre Dumas *fils*, 1848

"You will never love me thirty years. No one will."

Greta Garbo was the queen of romance, and after her turn as doomed Russian heroine *Anna Karenina* in 1935 she set her sights on portraying another tragic leading lady. Alexandre Dumas's 1848 novel *The Lady of the Camellias* was successful upon its publication and inspired a variety of stories, from operas to ballets, in addition to feature films. Dumas tells the love story between a courtesan named Marguerite Gautier (Garbo) and Armand Duval (Robert Taylor), a man who comes from a good though not wealthy family. They share a brief but torrid love affair that is threatened by Marguerite's past as well as her deteriorating health.

The illegitimate son and namesake of the acclaimed author of *The Count of Monte Cristo* and a dressmaker, Alexandre Dumas was referred to with the suffix *fils* at the end of his name to differentiate him from his famous father. When he was seven, his father legally recognized him, opening up access to wealth and education. But with this came loss, as the young Dumas was also removed from his mother's care. This separation caused

Alexandre Dumas *fils* to become fascinated with tragic, forgotten women, with some critics alleging the character of Marguerite Gautier was inspired by Dumas's mother. (The more direct inspiration for Camille and the courtesan Marguerite was Marie Duplessis, herself a courtesan, with whom Dumas fell in love when he was twenty.)

In the early 1850s, Dumas worked with Italian composer Giuseppe Fortunino Francesco Verdi on an operatic adaptation of the story that became the legendary opera *La traviata*. Later editions of the novel shortened the title to *Camille*. Hollywood began adapting the story starting in 1912, with subsequent versions in 1915 (starring Clara Kimball Young), 1917 (with Theda Bara), 1921 (with Alla Nazimova and Rudolph Valentino), and 1926 (with Norma Talmadge). A decade later, MGM—under the auspices of "boy wonder" producer Irving Thalberg—sought to give the mother of all lovelorn ladies to the elusive Greta Garbo. At the time of development, Thalberg thought that the morality of the day had evolved enough that Garbo portraying a sex worker wouldn't be shameful, though screenwriters James Hilton, Frances Marion (who also wrote the 1915 version), and Zoe Akins balanced out Marguerite Gautier's profession with an inner goodness and respectability that hewed closer to Anna Karenina than the more flawed and tolerated Marguerite from the book.

Dumas begins his story at the end of the romance, with Marguerite already dead from the consumption that has ravaged her body. An unnamed narrator opens the book by calling it a "testimony," asserting that the events are 100 percent true and that, if needed, he can provide witnesses. Displaying shades of the author himself, the narrator attends an auction of Marguerite's belongings, where he is introduced to the tall, blond Armand Duval, who shares the tragic love story with him—but not before a late-night trip to the cemetery to see Marguerite's exhumed corpse, which Armand believes he needs to see to prove that she's truly, most sincerely dead. Armand tells of meeting Marguerite, the origins of their romance, their attempt to live like normal people, and their eventual parting. Marguerite is perceived exclusively through Armand's eyes until their separation, after which the reader hears her voice strictly through letters she's written.

The 1936 feature is a more concise telling of Marguerite and Armand's love affair. The movie format—and Garbo's casting—places Marguerite firmly as the driving force and central protagonist of the narrative, although those who read the description of her on the page might be thrown by the casting of the Swedish actress as Marguerite, described as a girl of twenty with "jet black hair." The "most extravagant woman in Paris," as the film says, Marguerite lives fully in the present, spending her time at the theater and generally going from friend to friend in search of companionship and a place to stay. In the movie, Marguerite doesn't have an established home, and is reliant on reciprocal friendships to keep her afloat. Because the movie can only go so far with her role as a sex worker, it has a rather rose-colored view of courtesans at the time. Despite her profession, Marguerite is constantly in debt, so much so that when she's on her deathbed in the book, the creditors are literally in her house seizing her property.

The book is anchored by Armand, so Dumas reveals only as much of Marguerite's past as she shares with her lover, like her confession that she was illiterate and unable to write her name until "six years prior." Marguerite also divulges that her mother physically abused her, and admits to not weeping over her death. In fact, her tough childhood without love prompts

Marguerite to tell Armand that her love for him is akin to the love she feels for her dog. Marguerite is hesitant to start anything with Armand because, as she reiterates time and again, he will always be jealous because of what she does. Dumas also works with themes of jealousy and how a woman's past sins are always used against her no matter what her significant other says. Regardless, their relationship develops so quickly in the novel that it's almost laughable. They know each other for just two days before she agrees to become his mistress. It's unclear how much of this is motivated by love on Marguerite's end, versus desire for financial security.

Marguerite's fears soon come true. As she continues to ply her trade, Armand becomes obsessively worried about what she's doing and is jealous of everyone she encounters. Novels of this type often show the male lead trying to redeem the heroine through his love, and Armand thinks that if he can financially take care of Marguerite, she'll have no reason to continue working. He also thinks it will help her physically, ridding her of the consumption that wracks her body.

Marguerite agrees to leave her profession and take up residence in the country with Armand. Her consumption subsides, but unfortunately the pair can't seem to keep their heads above water financially. Armand tries to make money on his own, taking to gambling and dipping into his trust fund to support her. Marguerite, too proud to ask Armand for money, understands there's nowhere for their relationship to go, and as much as she wants to be with him, she enjoys having financial independence and living a lavish lifestyle. There is no route that doesn't involve her returning to her profession. Armand's father plays on Marguerite's true love for Armand in the movie and tells her to give him up in order to save her lover's reputation. This proposition is presented to her in a simple letter in the book.

On the page, Armand's father is less concerned about his son's reputation and more about his daughter's, who is soon to marry; the father fears Armand's sister will be abandoned by her fiancé because of the rumors about Armand and Marguerite.

Marguerite's decision to leave Armand varies with the formats. The movie shows her decision as a noble sacrifice, not unlike Garbo throwing herself in front of a train in *Anna Karenina*. But Armand is unable and unwilling to let the relationship end in the novel. He pursues Marguerite to Paris, believing she has abandoned him for a man with money. He proceeds to take up with another courtesan, named Olympe (Lenore Ulric)—shown in the movie as a snarky friend of Marguerite's—and proceeds to inflict what he calls "a continual persecution" against Marguerite, flaunting Olympe in front of her and writing Marguerite letters filled with "everything bitter, shameful, and cruel that I could think of." Part of Armand's recounting of this story, and his overwrought emotion at Marguerite's passing, stems from his guilt at how he treated her, not knowing the true backstory that she gave him up to spare him and his family a black mark on their name.

Producer Irving Thalberg called Garbo "the most memorable Camille of our time." Sadly, he didn't live to see the finished film, dying unexpectedly from pneumonia in September 1936. His early death mimicked Marguerite's own. Garbo was nominated for Best Actress at the 10th Academy Awards, losing out to Luise Rainer in *The Good Earth* (1937). *Camille* was adapted several times after this. Most famously, director Baz Luhrmann used it as inspiration for the 2001 jukebox musical *Moulin Rouge!*, the story of doomed courtesan Satine (Nicole Kidman) and her love for penniless writer Christian (Ewan McGregor).

GONE WITH THE WIND

1939

Directed by Victor Fleming
Screenplay by Sidney Howard
Based on *Gone with the Wind* by Margaret Mitchell, 1936

"Frankly my dear, I don't give a damn."

Margaret Mitchell's only novel, 1936's *Gone with the Wind*, is not just an iconic piece of literary history; it also serves as the foundation of one of the most widely recognizable films of all time. The story of spoiled Southern belle Scarlett O'Hara (Vivien Leigh) and her determination to save her family home, Tara, has been celebrated for decades by readers and critics for its themes of resilience and its depiction of the changing face of the South post–Civil War. But it is the tempestuous romance between Scarlett and the rascally Rhett Butler (Clark Gable) that has cemented the film's position as one of cinema's grandest love stories.

Mitchell wrote nine drafts of the novel, eight of which named the main character Prissy Hamilton, before she ultimately settled on the name Scarlett O'Hara. Scarlett is sixteen when the book starts and is described on the page as the most strong-willed of the O'Hara sisters, but not a great beauty (Vivien Leigh might be considered a glow-up for the character).

The reader learns that, as a child, Scarlett was a tomboy content to climb trees, who eventually gave that up to feign helplessness and silliness to attract men.

Ironically, Hollywood was not champing at the bit to adapt the movie prior to publication. Every studio in town declined to pursue an adaptation. Darryl F. Zanuck of Twentieth Century Fox originally turned down the rights, only to have his mind changed by story editor Kay Brown and business partner John Hay Whitney. He eventually paid $50,000 (approximately $1.2 million today) for the rights. George Cukor was tasked with directing, but after clashes with Clark Gable, director Victor Fleming was brought on. Fleming soon had a nervous breakdown and briefly left the project. The directorial merry-go-round, coupled with a budget spiraling out of control, saw the movie labeled "Selznick's Folly" until its premiere in 1939.

It's no surprise that the role of Scarlett O'Hara was the most coveted one of the 1930s, with several top actresses vying for it. Katharine Hepburn was said to have wanted it desperately, and everyone from Jean Arthur to Lana Turner was considered. Mitchell did not want to say who she'd prefer in the role, but she disclosed that *Design for Living* (1933) actress Miriam Hopkins was her top choice for Scarlett and Basil Rathbone was her preferred Rhett Butler.

Many different hands touched *Gone with the Wind*'s script, including Ben Hecht, Jo Swerling, and John Van Druten. Mitchell's novel is nearly one thousand pages, and while the finished film clocks in at nearly four hours, much was condensed from the original story, including nixing extended histories for Scarlett's father Gerald (Thomas Mitchell) and Rhett Butler. In the novel, Gerald is said to have fled Ireland after killing a man in a feud. He soon secured his first slave and plantation in a poker game, amassing the wealth (and Tara) that

Scarlett grew up with. Once the war breaks out, Rhett Butler's role on a blockade runner, bringing in supplies to an isolated Atlanta, also gets extended page time as he helps the citizens of Georgia gain access to essential items while simultaneously profiting himself. Other characters, like planter's son Tony Fontaine, Tara's "man of the house" Will Benteen, Rhett's sister Rosemary, and Scarlett's lawyer Henry Hamilton take up space and plot in the book but aren't retained in the movie. Their absence does detract from the latter, especially that of Will Benteen, who specifically puts the spotlight on Mitchell's "happy" house slaves in the novel.

Scarlett herself has a more succinct plotline in the film. The reader sees her hastily become the child bride of Charles Hamilton and give birth to a son, Wade Hampton. Charles later dies of pneumonia caused by measles before ever seeing battle. Later, during her second marriage, to Frank Kennedy, she gives birth to a daughter, Ella Lorena, who Scarlett thinks is ugly. The point of Scarlett's declaration is that Ella and Wade resemble their fathers, men Scarlett doesn't love. Neither child has much of a plot in the book. It isn't until she gives birth to her child with Rhett, Eugenie Victoria ("Bonnie Blue"), that her role as a mother is examined in depth, though Scarlett is a fairly hands-off parent—Rhett says in book and movie that "a cat is a better mother than [Scarlett]"—not surprising, considering we see Scarlett effectively raised by house slave Mammy (Hattie

McDaniel). Bonnie becomes the one thing that keeps Rhett and Scarlett together.

The relationship between Rhett and Scarlett plays out similarly in the book, though Rhett's relationship with sex worker Belle Watling (Ona Munson) is sanitized on-screen compared to their relationship in the novel. In the book, Belle bears a son she names Tazewell Butler. It's never explicitly said whether the child is Rhett's, but he adopts the boy as his ward and sends him away to be educated. If you're curious about Rhett's famous farewell line in the movie, that originated in the book, albeit lacking the "frankly." (Despite claims to the contrary, this was not the first time the word "damn" was heard in film; that distinction goes to 1938's *Pygmalion*.)

Both versions have been criticized since release for their now dated and offensive portrayal of African Americans. Mitchell's novel never acknowledges how the O'Haras and other wealthy plantation owners built their business on oppression. House slaves like Mammy and Prissy (Butterfly McQueen) are smiling, happy, and resistant to ending their slavery or refusing to abandon the O'Haras at any point. Mitchell describes the lives of Black people in this time as one of positivity and casts their hardships as the result of an inability to care for themselves. The film doesn't go into detail on the interior lives of Mammy and others, but presents similar ideas. The book also explores the Ku Klux Klan, written as an organization whose goal it is to protect white people from unruly Black people. Both Ashley Wilkes (Leslie Howard) and Scarlett's second husband, Frank, are Klansmen, but Ashley is "against violence of any sort." Ultimately it is Rhett who ends up disbanding the local chapter.

Gone with the Wind became, and remains, the highest-grossing film of all time, amassing $4.3 billion (adjusted for inflation). The movie also won eight Academy Awards, including Best Picture, Best Actress (Vivien Leigh), Best Supporting Actress (Hattie McDaniel, who was not only the first Black actress to win but also the first to be nominated), Best Director for Victor Fleming, and Best Screenplay. Mitchell won the Pulitzer Prize in 1937, but she wasn't happy about the book's massive success nor did she appreciate being in the spotlight. She continued writing, but strictly in the nonfiction space. Regardless, Scarlett O'Hara's loss of Rhett Butler due to her own pride and ignorance, seen in the book and the movie, continues to enthrall audiences to this day. Rhett Butler didn't give a damn, but we sure do.

PRIDE AND PREJUDICE

1940

Directed by Robert Z. Leonard
Screenplay by Aldous Huxley and Jane Murfin
Based on *Pride and Prejudice* by Jane Austen, 1813

"I've walked the streets of London reminding myself of the unsuitability of such a marriage. Ah, the obstacles between us. But, it won't do. I can struggle against you no longer."

Jane Austen's novel *Pride and Prejudice* has inspired countless directors and creatives since its publication in 1813, from straightforward adaptations of the book to more free-spirited takes like Kevin Kwan's novel *Crazy Rich Asians* (less so that book's 2018 film adaptation) and Joel Kim Booster's queer romance film *Fire Island* (2022). It's impossible to think of a world where hardheaded heroine Elizabeth Bennett and the equally stubborn Fitzwilliam Darcy aren't the definitive portrait of romance. Their "enemies to lovers" plotline is formulaic now but remains fresh and inventive in the novel as the reader sees the pair grow and overcome their own adversities to find love. Surprisingly, it wasn't until the 1940 MGM adaptation of the movie that interest in Austen's book grew to what it is today.

"It is a truth universally acknowledged, that a single man in possession of good fortune, must be in want of a wife," writes Austen in her famous opening line. This implies that the story focuses exclusively on marriage, but it's one of numerous moments that set up *Pride and Prejudice* as a social satire. The story of Lizzie Bennett and her four sisters sees them navigate through Regency-era England, a culturally fruitful time from 1795 to 1837, negotiating the social mores of the period while in search of a husband. Austen uses this to explore everything from class consciousness to the reduced circumstances of women of the era. A key plot point sees Elizabeth compelled to marry the boring clergyman Mr. Collins due to England's law of entailment, which forced a landowner to bequeath property to the nearest living male relative, often leaving wives and daughters penniless.

Mr. Darcy, a member of the upper class, makes his pride evident upon first meeting with Elizabeth, offering demeaning remarks about her without realizing she can hear him, and it is her eventual prejudice toward him—reliant on the information of others—that puts them at odds throughout the novel. Austen compels the reader to make their own decisions about the characters while reading. She also wants the reader to craft a perception of them through their dialogue, so there's little physical description of the characters, making them ripe for a Hollywood producer to cast the characters how they please.

The hope was to adapt Austen's novel alongside a string of other costume dramas and literary adaptations that culminated with *Gone with the Wind* and *Rebecca* (1940). In 1936, MGM's Irving Thalberg made plans to adapt the book with his wife, Norma Shearer, as Elizabeth and Clark Gable as Darcy.

Thalberg's death in September of that year put the brakes on things until 1939, when director George Cukor became attached to the project with Robert Donat as Darcy. Director Robert Z. Leonard, who'd previously helmed *The Great Ziegfeld* (1936) and several Jeanette McDonald musicals, was hired after Cukor left, and it was Leonard who put the film in front of cameras. Melvyn Douglas, Robert Taylor, and Errol Flynn were considered for Darcy before Laurence Olivier was hired. *Pride and Prejudice* came out just three months after Olivier's turn in Hitchcock's *Rebecca*. Olivier campaigned hard for his lover—and eventual wife—Vivien Leigh to play Lizzie, but it was Greer Garson, Louis B. Mayer's protégée and perceived successor to grand dame Norma Shearer, who got the role. At thirty-six, Garson was the oldest actor to portray Elizabeth "Lizzie" Bennett, who is about twenty in the book.

Because Austen's text has so many deep-rooted themes regarding class distinctions, screenwriters Aldous Huxley (who also wrote the adaptation of Charlotte Brontë's *Jane Eyre* three years later) and Jane Murfin focused on translating Helen Jerome's stage adaptation, as opposed to Austen's text. What results is a light, frothy costume drama sold by the studio as a romantic comedy. The film's tagline is "Bachelors Beware! Five Gorgeous Beauties Are on a Madcap Hunt." Gone is the Regency setting, where much of the social satire and rules make sense, in favor of moving it to a later time "in OLD ENGLAND" as the opening text crawl says. This change was presumably fueled to allow for more expansive and eye-catching costumes compared to the slimmer, flowy gowns worn during the actual time period. The average viewer might think the book takes place in the antebellum South rather than England (a fact not helped by many of the props and costumes being recycled from *Gone with the Wind*).

The movie plays like a *Cliff's Notes* version of the story, with every major character introduced within the film's first scene or two, including the villainous Mr. Wickham (Edward Ashley). The movie's focus surrounds the eventual marriage of Garson's Lizzie and Olivier's Darcy, with a side plot devoted to Lizzie's older sister Jane (Maureen O'Sullivan) and her love for Mr. Bingley (Bruce Lester).

Other changes were meant to appease the Hays Code, specifically transforming Mr. Collins (Melville Cooper) from a clergyman into a librarian so as not to criticize religion. Interestingly, the humor derived from Mr. Collins in the book isn't due to his being a clergyman but rather his snobbery toward the lower class. This snobbery is in spite of the fact that he is higher ranked only by his association with Darcy's aunt, Lady Catherine de Bourgh (Edna May Oliver).

Oliver's Lady Catherine, one of the last impediments to Darcy and Lizzie's romance, is a comic archetype in the movie who demands that Lizzie promise to not marry Darcy, threatening to disinherit him. This threat is played as a test to see whether Lizzie is a fortune hunter in the book, but it is very much a serious demand from Lady Catherine on-screen.

One assumes the novel's climax is Darcy's proposal to Elizabeth, but that moment is actually anticlimactic, with Lizzie's response just a brief paragraph. The novel's ending explains what happened to the various other couples around them. The movie simply concludes with Darcy and Lizzie's happy ending.

In the book, Lizzie and Darcy take the Shakespearean "opposites attract" plotline to its inevitable conclusion, with the pair understanding how to compromise for each other. The film versions simply see them realizing they're perfect for each other, and that's enough.

Despite grossing $1.9 million at the box office, *Pride and Prejudice* lost MGM $240,000. Mayer used the movie as an example against adapting classic literature in the future. One person who benefited posthumously from the movie was Jane Austen, with five different editions of the novel coming out to coincide with the release, eventually going through twenty-one printings by the 1950s. Despite Mayer's proclamation, MGM considered adapting it again in 1947 as a musical but scrapped that idea. It continued to be adapted, however, most famously as a 1995 television miniseries version for the BBC starring Jennifer Ehle as Lizzie and Colin Firth as Darcy, and comprising nearly the entirety of the book; and in 2005 director Joe Wright adapted it with Keira Knightley as Elizabeth. That film has become beloved in its own right for its swoony tone and is now considered the de facto adaptation of the story.

RANDOM HARVEST

1942

Directed by Mervyn LeRoy
Screenplay by Claudine West,
George Froeschel, and Arthur Wimperis
Based on *Random Harvest* by James Hilton, 1941

"Smithy?"

A man missing his memory walks out of a mental hospital the same day World War I ends. He goes to buy cigarettes when he comes upon a beautiful stranger. Fearing he'll be sent back to the hospital, the woman takes pity on him and helps hide him in the hopes of getting him back on his feet. Greer Garson is the woman, Paula Ridgeway, and Ronald Colman is the man with no memory, known only as "Smithy," Paula's pet name for him. The couple falls in love, only to have that shattered when Smithy eventually regains his memory, and forgets Paula in the process. Thus begins director Mervyn LeRoy's 1942 adaptation of James Hilton's *Random Harvest*, a story of love's endurance over time and how it's impossible to erase the memory of one's soulmate.

Hilton's novel plays around with structure, presenting Smithy and Paula's relationship in flashback. MGM's film lays out the story chronologically. Smith leaves the mental institution and meets Paula. The two try to stay one step ahead of those who want him back at the hospital. The couple marries and has a son, but when Smith is hit by a cab and remembers who he is, the movie's second half is about him reintegrating into his former life as Charles Rainier. The audience is left to wonder what happened to Paula and how the two will find each other again. The audience understands that Paula is where Rainier's true happiness lies, and the entire story is about how the pair will eventually reunite.

In the novel, a young man named Harrison, Rainier's secretary, learns about Rainier's memory lapse and how he is missing two years of his life. Rainier recalls waking up on a Liverpool park bench and being shocked to hear World War I has ended. Charles recounts everything to Harrison from that point forward: how he returned to the Rainier family home, only to find himself declared legally dead and his father dying. After his father dies, Charles's eldest brother Chet, heir to the Rainier fortune, squanders everything and forces Charles to give up his education at Cambridge to save the business. The reader comes to understand Charles's life and how unhappy and isolated he is. He's clearly missing something, not just his memories, that would make him feel fulfilled.

MGM had already seen massive success with another Hilton adaptation, 1939's *Goodbye, Mr. Chips*, and snapped up the rights for $50,000 with hopes of having Spencer Tracy in the role. But Colman's mix of aristocratic bearing, well suited to the scenes where Charles is playing a wealthy man, and his sensitive romantic charm makes him perfect for Smith and complements Garson's maternal Paula. Coupled with the release of *The Talk of the Town* the same year, *Random Harvest* returned Colman to prominence while showing that, even pushing fifty, he still had the ability to be a romantic leading man. (Garson was thirteen years younger than Colman.) Hilton himself was incredibly pleased at how the script changed his book.

Where Hilton's novel gives an air of mystery to the romance, with Charles trying to figure out his past and find the identity of the woman he truly loved, the movie is a story of watching the pair find their way back together. The movie makes their fates certain, while the book teases the reader about whether Charles will find his soulmate.

The book and movie play with duality and how people are different around others, especially romantic partners. Charles is different from Smithy, and Paula—her stage name—is different from Margaret Hanson, her legal name. The joy of both book and film is discovering how each person's identity melds both halves of who they are. Paula searches for Smithy while mourning the death of their infant son, who has died under unknown circumstances after Smithy's disappearance. She takes on work as a secretary, sees Charles—her Smithy—in the newspaper, and gets a job as his executive secretary using her real name. Watching the film, it's only a matter of time before they're reunited.

But the book, being told in the present, introduces Charles as already married to a woman named Helen, his former secretary, whom others criticize for her lavish parties. The reader wonders, if Charles finds Paula, how he'll be with her as a married man. The reveal of Helen as Paula is a surprise, as she is placed in the same shadowy position as Charles and Harrison. It makes the ending even sweeter, however, that even without recognizing her, Charles's heart knew there was something special and married her anyway.

Garson made her cinematic debut in Hilton's *Goodbye, Mr. Chips*. The release of *Random Harvest*, put out six months after her other wartime weepy, *Mrs. Miniver* (1942), saw the studio dub it "the year of Greer." The success of both films made her the queen of the MGM lot. Though she wasn't nominated for her role in this film, she still won an Academy Award for *Mrs. Miniver.*

Random Harvest was made during the first full year of World War II, but you wouldn't know it in the movie when Smithy and Paula meet on Armistice Day of World War I. To show the timeless nature of their romance, there is nothing to denote when events take place in the movie. It's assumed the film concludes around 1935, before the start of World War II. This offers the lovers, and the audience, a brief respite from the horrors of another impending war.

By contrast, Hilton is very much interested in the war in the novel when Rainier and Paula meet at the end of World War I, concluding the book with the announcement of Hitler invading Poland in 1939. Harrison wonders if he'll be drafted, while Charles's awareness that Paula and Helen are one and the same gives readers the ability to believe the couple will be able to survive this second war; they have each other to cling to in the face of such uncertainty.

Hilton's novel is denser than LeRoy's film, but both tell a sweet, tempered story of memory. What do we know in our bones, even if we aren't aware of why? It ultimately shows how true love is impossible to forget.

JANE EYRE

1943

Directed by Robert Stevenson
Screenplay by Aldous Huxley,
Robert Stevenson, and John Houseman
Based on *Jane Eyre* by Charlotte Brontë, 1847

"Do you think because I'm poor and obscure and plain that I'm soulless and heartless?"

Charlotte Brontë's *Jane Eyre* has thrilled and dazzled audiences for its blend of timeless romance and Gothic suspense since its initial publication in 1847. The story follows the titled heroine as she grows up under harsh and loveless conditions to become a governess at Thornfield Hall, a manor house owned by the brooding and mysterious Edward Rochester.

With the novel's blend of romance and ghostly thrills, Hollywood had already adapted it multiple times during the silent era, as well as a 1934 version starring Virginia Bruce as Jane and a post-*Frankenstein* (1931) Colin Clive as Rochester. That film was critically panned upon release for Bruce's far-from-plain Jane and for its lighter tone. So, in 1943, under the eye of Twentieth Century Fox, Brontë's *Jane Eyre* got another adaptation that doesn't tell the complete story but hews closer to the original mood. Fox's version owes its life to Alfred

Hitchcock's *Rebecca*, itself a Gothic-esque romantic costume drama written by a female author. The movies are both dark and evocative and also share the same leading lady: Joan Fontaine. There are also similarities found here to the 1939 film adaptation of Brontë's sister Emily's book *Wuthering Heights*. Rochester's violent and aggressive nature, coupled with a suffering history, has much in common with *Wuthering Heights*'s tormented Heathcliffe, and Fontaine's Jane has some of the same fiery spirit as Catherine Earnshaw (played in *Wuthering Heights* by Merle Oberon), but it's dampened in comparison with the character on the page.

The movie's main claim to fame is the brief appearance by a ten-year-old Elizabeth Taylor, who had just signed a twelve-month contract with MGM and was immediately loaned out to Fox. In the brief role as Helen Burns, Jane's only childhood friend, who dies during an outbreak of typhus, Taylor is extraordinarily magnetic, even if she doesn't quite convey the character's extreme piousness.

Charlotte Brontë wrote Jane much like herself. Brontë had also lost a parent—her mother, at the age of five. She and her siblings were sent to Cowan Bridge School, where tuberculosis killed two of Brontë's sisters, Maria and Elizabeth, just as Jane's friend Helen dies at Lowood School. Jane's debaucherous cousin John Reed, an alcoholic, mimics Brontë's brother, Branwell. Brontë even spent time as a governess for the wealthy Sedgwick family, a job she personally hated, just as Jane acts as governess to Rochester's ward, Adèle.

Jane Eyre is a bildungsroman—a story where the reader sees the protagonist develop physically and mentally—so the book tracks Jane from her childhood through to adulthood and her meeting with Rochester, and their eventual wedding. The movie is faithful for much of the story, showcasing young Jane's (Peggy Anne Garner) time living with her aunt Mrs. Reed (Agnes Moorehead) and her time at Lowood. When Jane grows into Joan Fontaine, the movie takes us to the Thornfield estate, where it focuses exclusively on the relationship between Jane and Rochester.

Because of the desire to tell a straightforward romance, much of the novel's gender dynamics are absent. Critics have argued that Jane is a protofeminist for her back-and-forth longing for love and freedom. The book sees Jane show concern for how marrying Rochester limits her autonomy and could tie her down. Jane is in a gray area socially; she isn't a servant but is still an employee of Rochester's. She isn't common, yet she isn't an aristocrat. Jane worries marriage would cement her into a lower position and make her inferior.

Like the earlier *Wuthering Heights* film, which removes the novel's entire second half, the 1943 interpretation of *Jane Eyre* deletes the book's third act, which details what happens after Jane leaves Thornfield upon the reveal of Rochester's wife, Bertha Mason—a woman never seen on screen but played up as a snarling, grabbing monster—who lives in the manor's attic due to her uncontrollable madness. Jane flees Thornfield with no job or money, and literally falls on the doorstep of the Rivers family, consisting of the pious missionary St. John and his two sisters. St. John is determined to marry Jane, insisting that by refusing him she's refusing faith in Christianity itself. It is then that Jane, compelled by Rochester's disembodied voice on the breeze, returns to Thornfield and marries him.

At the time, the movie was hyped more for having Orson Welles in the role of Rochester, fresh off his run in *Citizen Kane* (1941), *The Magnificent Ambersons* (1942), and *Journey into Fear* (1943). Welles performed the character in 1940 for a radio adaptation and decided to do the film under the condition that he'd get top billing, a Moviola camera to film his own projects on his downtime, and an associate producer credit. All of his demands were accommodated, except for the credit. Welles hoped to use the money he made from *Jane Eyre* to finance his Latin American omnibus feature *It's All True*. Sadly, that movie never came to fruition.

The film's Rochester is sanitized from the novel. On the page, Rochester admits to Jane that he engaged in flagrant promiscuity as he tried to find a woman to love him after his disastrous relationship with Bertha. He confesses to an affair with the mother of his ward, Adèle (Margaret O'Brien), but denies being the child's father. Welles plays it as if he is begrudgingly kind enough to care for the child knowing he isn't related to her, whereas the book insinuates that Rochester is lying.

Jane and Rochester's dynamic is also softened from the book. Gone is Jane's fear that Rochester only sees her as a plaything for his own whims. The movie plays it as a romance of class differences, with Fontaine's Jane a shy, meek governess to the more powerful and commanding Rochester. Brontë ends *Jane Eyre* with the pair's marriage, but all of this is meant as a reward for Jane's goodness and resilience. The book posits Jane as an example of a good woman, one who suffers trials and tribulations and is rewarded with a man. Rochester ends up blind at the end, after Bertha sets Thornfield on fire, and this plays as ironic: He is literally blind now but was emotionally blind to Jane's love for him previously. He is redeemed for his bad behavior and his sordid past and is now able to give his love to Jane wholeheartedly.

Jane Eyre was remade several times for both film and television after 1943. The most recent version, from 2011, sees Mia Wasikowska as Jane and Michael Fassbender as Rochester. This version is more faithful to the novel and comprises the entirety of the story, including the Rivers plotline. (Funnily enough, neither the 2011 nor the 1943 version includes the fact that when Bertha Mason burns down Thornfield and Rochester is blinded trying to save her, he also loses a hand. The Rochesters in both 2011 and 1943 are blind, but keep their hands.)

LAURA

1944

Directed by Otto Preminger
Screenplay by Jay Dratler, Samuel Hoffenstein, and Elizabeth Reinhardt
Based on *Laura* by Vera Caspary, 1943

"I shall never forget the weekend Laura died."

At the beginning of Otto Preminger's 1944 romantic noir, *Laura*, the visage of the exquisite Laura Hunt (Gene Tierney) is the first face the viewer sees, encapsulated in an oil painting of Tierney's beautiful face, which fills the frame. The opening line, spoken by Laura's friend Waldo Lydecker (Clifton Webb), tells us something straight off: She is dead and, in theory, isn't ever coming back. As David Raskin's swoony score plays over the opening credits, the audience goes on a journey toward discovering who Laura Hunt was, and why she was killed.

Detective Mark McPherson (Dana Andrews) is tasked with handling the case and interviews people in Laura's life, specifically the effete newspaper columnist, Waldo, and Laura's fiancé, Shelby Carpenter (Vincent Price). But as Mark starts to learn more about the enigmatic woman, he realizes his own growing love for her.

Vera Caspary, a Chicago-born stenographer turned author and screenwriter, laid the foundation for the noirish romance with her 1943 book. Whereas the film is a story about the many loves of Laura, Caspary's book is a story about a woman's love for her independence and the line between romance and obsession. Caspary's work often focused on female characters who struggle to obtain personal freedom through employment. Laura Hunt is a successful ad executive, not unlike Caspary herself. Caspary's heroines aren't "victimized dames," as A. B. Emerys writes in a 2005 piece on the author, nor are they "rescued damsels" either. Caspary was inspired to write *Laura* after hearing about a woman killed in a gas explosion that destroyed her face. Caspary mimics this, somewhat, with the nude body found in Laura's penthouse. A shotgun blast from her murderer has obliterated her face. But when Laura turns up alive and well it's discovered that the murdered girl is model Diane Redfern, whom Laura knows as Shelby's lover.

Much of Laura's conflict in the book is over whether to marry Shelby at all. It isn't his philandering that bothers her, but the sense of confinement she believes comes with marriage. Laura routinely questions in diary entries in the book what she will have to sacrifice if she marries Shelby, seeing marriage as meaning giving up her job and independence. This feeling is especially poignant since Shelby is depicted in the book as a Southern gentleman who wants his wife to stay home. In contrast, Vincent Price gives a more sophisticated performance; even when he is caught courting more than one woman, his charm overcomes everything. Once Laura returns from the dead—actually a visit to her country estate—in the movie, the mystery becomes who would want to kill her, and not necessarily about finding justice for Diane, killed in a case of mistaken identity. Diane was a woman in love with Shelby, and, much like Laura, she was let down by him. To Caspary, though, Diane is another victim in a world where, for all men's talk of love, they mistreat women cruelly. Mark says girls like Diane are a "dime a dozen," but they are not to the author. She devotes significant time in the book to describing who Diane was as a person. Mark travels to Diane's apartment and learns about how she worked in a New Jersey mill while caring for her mother before she moved to New York. He discovers her name is fake; her real name is Jenny Swobodo. Caspary makes the case that the story is just as much Diane's as Laura's, but Laura has more people who are interested in her.

Caspary's book isn't anti-romance, though it aims at being more pragmatic in its depiction of love compared to the movie. Caspary plays with narrative point of view in the novel to show how different people in relationships see others, whether that's Waldo presenting himself as entitled to possess Laura under the guise of love, or Mark being clumsy and awkward in relationships. The first section of the book is told from Waldo's point of view, akin to an article or book he wants to write. Later in the novel, Mark says that he isn't a writer so his words aren't as lovely and florid as Waldo's, a metaphor for his courting of Laura.

Waldo controls the facts of his relationship with Laura. His being a writer brings an air of authenticity to his story. He is the first to make the reader question how perspective changes things by saying, "I offer the narrative, not so much as a detective yarn as a love story. I wish I were its hero." Physically, Caspary's Waldo is a far cry from Clifton Webb. She describes him as an overweight epileptic, an outdated element of the book meant to present him as an unattractive man unworthy of Laura's love.

When Laura becomes the prime suspect in Diane's murder, it's up to Mark to clear her name, which he does in both film and book. Laura falls for him, and though the happy ending of Caspary's book can feel pat—will Mark allow her to continue working?—it's part of the author's exploration of the era. Women of the 1940s were often torn between love and independence, working and raising families. Laura's diary pages in the novel give the reader insight into the "real" Laura, one who is imperfect, petty, and has sexual desires. Her attraction to Shelby makes her extremely jealous of Diane Redfern. Waldo reveals that after seeing Shelby and Diane together at a cocktail party, Laura became so angry she hit Diane with an hors d'oeuvre tray in a jealous rage. Laura understands that she will have to give something up no matter what, and she chooses love, or at least lust, at the end.

Caspary wasn't too happy with Preminger's numerous changes to her story, particularly the casting of Tierney in the title role. The author derogatorily referred to Tierney's depiction of Laura as a "Hollywood version of a cute career girl." Her biggest complaint against the movie was the ending, which concludes with Waldo revealed as the murderer. He returns to Laura's apartment to kill her with the shotgun he's stashed in her grandfather clock. In the book, Waldo carries the murder weapon with him throughout the entire story in the form of a sawed-off shotgun that looks like a walking stick. Preminger didn't believe the stick would look convincing and thus went with the grandfather clock, hearkening back to Waldo's love of antiques in the book. Producer Darryl Zanuck also didn't like the ending with the shotgun in the clock, wishing the entire thing had been made up in Waldo's head. This change was said to have been filmed and presented in a screening attended by gossip columnist Walter Winchell. When Winchell told Zanuck, "I didn't get [the ending]. You have to change it," the ending was left as it remains in the movie.

Laura saw several iterations after its release in 1944. It was most famously remade as a 1968 movie starring Lee Radziwill (credited as Lee Bouvier) as Laura, George Sanders as Waldo, and Robert Stack as Mark. Despite the casting and a script by Truman Capote, the film was universally panned. It's understandable; like its heroine, *Laura* is a hard story to tell again.

Its role in the film noir canon—cited as a leading example of the then new genre of film noir in 1946—is indisputable and irreplaceable. Although Caspary wasn't happy with the movie, it works as a unique companion to her novel. The movie tells a moody, dark story of two people brought together by obsession who find true romance in each other, while the book tells of one woman's love for herself and coming to understand what love looks like to her.

DRAGONWYCK

1946

Directed by Joseph L. Mankiewicz
Screenplay by Joseph L. Mankiewicz
Based on *Dragonwyck* by Anya Seton, 1944

"The breeze must feel wonderful indeed with a face as beautiful as yours against it."

The best Gothic romances have a spooky old house and a deep ancestral legacy with which an outsider heroine comes in to do battle. Such is the case with Anya Seton's 1944 novel *Dragonwyck*, which follows the eighteen-year-old Miranda Wells (Gene Tierney), a teenage girl living in Connecticut in 1844. Miranda dreams of a life of luxury and excitement, which is at odds with her overly religious farm upbringing. When her mother's estranged cousin Nicholas Van Ryn (Vincent Price) asks the Wellses to send one of their daughters to his ancestral estate, Dragonwyck, as a governess to his child, Miranda is the one chosen. Once there, Miranda doesn't just fall in love with the Van Ryn way of life, but with Nicholas himself.

Gothic romances tend to emulate each other, so it's unsurprising that Anya Seton—born in the 1920s—leans heavily on pre-established literary heroines, like the titular Jane Eyre from Charlotte Brontë's book and the second Mrs. De Winter from Daphne du Maurier's *Rebecca*, as inspiration for the character of Miranda. As with most female leads of the Gothic romance canon, Miranda starts out as a flighty, materialistic young woman—as opposed to someone who is just isolated and innocent—so much so that she's said to make her skin whiter by using buttermilk and cucumber poultices. Miranda despises getting her hands dirty, a common problem living on a farm, and grows to see her family as commoners. Dragonwyck is the life Miranda believes she is owed and she takes pride in catching Nicholas's eye, believing herself a far worthier wife for him than Johanna (Vivienne Osborne), whom he is already married to.

The novel focuses on Miranda's forbidden love for Nicholas not only as a matter of sexual attraction, but as an affair with a married man. Their romance and marriage becomes a battle of good versus evil for Miranda's soul. (Miranda is religious, whereas Nicholas is an atheist.) Nicholas sees himself as the master of his land, of others, and of himself, while Miranda learns to be her own independent woman.

Nicholas is a dark-haired, broody man who comes from old money. He is a patroon, one of the Hudson Valley area landowners who rents out his land to farmworkers who pay him tribute every month. Nicholas and Miranda's romance is set against the dissolution of the patroon system, which Nicholas refuses to acknowledge even when it becomes law. Coming from money, as well as having deep ancestral roots to the land and the old way of life, Nicholas's madness manifests as a belief that he can do whatever he wants, that he is near godlike. This comes to a head when, during a night at the theater, Nicholas and Miranda step

into the middle of a riot. Nicholas has a bucket of water dumped over him and, in anger, grabs a rifle and kills a young boy.

Taking similar inspiration from the film versions of *Jane Eyre* and *Rebecca*, *Dragonwyck* cuts the deeper themes of religion in favor of a straightforward Gothic romance between the naive Miranda and the overbearing, frightening Nicholas. As played by Tierney in the movie, Miranda is a bright-eyed innocent who stumbles upon the realization that Nicholas murdered Johanna. By the time Nicholas's true nature is revealed—he rapes Miranda on their wedding night—it's a "be careful what you wish for" moment in the book compared to the movie, in which she is a poor girl seduced and duped by a man who hid who he was.

Vincent Price was not Twentieth Century Fox's first choice for Nicholas. When director Ernest Lubitsch planned to direct *Dragonwyck*, he wanted Gregory Peck. But when Lubitsch took ill during preproduction, Peck dropped out, so Twentieth Century contract players Price and Tierney took the leads, reteaming after successful pairings in *Laura* (1944) and *Leave Her to Heaven* (1945). Price threads the needle between brooding and outright madness, between villain and romantic leading man, but with less of the character work seen in the novel.

The movie ends with Nicholas driven mad by a ghostly entity that has far more significance in the book. Seton reveals the story of Azilde Marie de la Courbet, Nicholas's great-grandmother: The prized "New Orleans belle" became a shell of her former self after marrying into the Van Ryn clan and eventually killed herself, acting as a cautionary tale for Miranda if she doesn't leave Dragonwyck forever.

In the book, Nicholas dies because of his own pride. Obsessed with steamboat racing, he and Miranda end up in a speed competition with another boat. The boat catches on fire due to the exertion and Nicholas saves Miranda, as well as a mother and her son on the same boat, before eventually drowning; his body is never found. His decision in his final moments proved "to himself and others that he was master after all . . ." Nicholas is hailed as a hero, albeit the reader knows his true personality. Miranda remarries the kindhearted country doctor Jeff Turner (Glenn Langan) and, being Nicholas's heir, she gets everything. But because she now understands material possessions aren't important—and wanting no connection to Nicholas at all—she refuses to accept anything and gives it all to Nicholas's and Johanna's daughter, Katrine (Connie Marshall), with the exception of Dragonwyck, which is razed to the ground.

Seton continued to write until 1975, and passed away at the age of eighty-six in 1990. While both versions of *Dragonwyck* come off as derivative of other works, it holds a special place for being an elegant, fascinating story of dark romance and the inner evil inside all of us.

THE BISHOP'S WIFE

1947

Directed by Henry Koster
Screenplay by Robert E. Sherwood and Leonardo Bercovici
Based on *The Bishop's Wife* by Robert Nathan, 1928

"When an Immortal finds himself envying the Mortal he is entrusted to his care, it's a danger signal."

The Bishop's Wife has been a Christmas classic since its release in 1947. The film tells the story of put-upon bishop Henry Brougham (David Niven), who asks for spiritual guidance to help get funding for a cathedral. Said guidance comes in the form of an angel named Dudley (Cary Grant), who tries to help Henry achieve his goal while reminding the bishop to appreciate what he has in life, including his lonely wife Julia (Loretta Young).

Screenwriters Robert E. Sherwood and Leonardo Bercovici (with some uncredited help from Billy Wilder and Charles Brackett) craft a whimsical narrative that, through Henry Koster's direction, has all the magic of something directed by French filmmaker and fellow fan of magical romance René Clair, who helmed *I Married a Witch* (1942). Add in Cary Grant as the utterly charming and swoon-worthy Dudley and it's no surprise that *The Bishop's Wife* is now a holiday staple and instant classic.

After the success of the Bing Crosby/Ingrid Bergman feature *The Bells of St. Mary's* (1945), producer Samuel Goldwyn sought to copy that popularity and went in search of his own movie with a heartwarming and inspirational message centered around the Christmas season. Goldwyn looked to the novels of author Robert Nathan. Goldwyn thought Nathan's 1928 novella, *The Bishop's Wife*, would be perfect. His 1933 book *One More Spring* was made into a film of the same name in 1935, and in 1946 his novel *The Enchanted Voyage* was translated into the film *Wake Up and Dream*.

But where the film crafts a love story swathed in the small-town Americana and the unifying spirit coming out of World War II, its source material is a satire that reflects on the 1920s hedonism leading up to the stock market crash of 1929. Nathan even pokes fun at the spiritual state of America during this period, saying in the opening lines that "In the schools, children were taught that four is twice as large as two; and to despise foreigners. As a result there emerged from the schoolrooms of the nation a race of men and women filled with pride, and anxious to increase two into four. Nothing was allowed to stand in the way of this ambition."

Because of the novel's sardonic tone and themes, it was tough to adapt. And yet, once the script was done, putting the movie in front of cameras wasn't any easier. The original plan was for Niven to play the angel, with Dana Andrews and Teresa Wright to star as Henry and Julia (a reteam for the couple after their performance in 1946's *The Best Years of Our Lives*). When Wright became unavailable, Andrews was lent to RKO to bring in Loretta Young as Julia and filming started with Cary

Grant now in the Andrews role. But after two weeks Goldwyn replaced director William A. Seiter with Henry Koster to refilm everything, and Grant and Niven had their roles swapped. It's unclear to this day whether Grant pushed to play Dudley or not. It's said the cost of finding a new director, scrapping the script in order to accommodate Grant and Niven switching roles, and the sets came out to $900,000.

In the book, Nathan tells the story of bishop Henry Brougham, a big-city bishop who dreams of crafting a "magnificent" cathedral to get more people into his church. The cathedral would stand as a testament to his skill. He seeks an archdeacon "compounded of equal parts of piety, tact, energy, and ability," and is visited by the angel, who is named Michael in the book. Unlike in the film, this iteration of Henry not only believes immediately in Michael's heavenly bona fides, but wants to tell his congregation about the visitation straightaway. (Michael says to do so would cause people to spend so much time in "prayer and contemplation" that society would crumble to worship at his feet.)

Suffice it to say, Nathan's Michael holds little in common with Grant's performance of the character. Where Grant is warm and balances the character's heavenly and mortal sides, Michael speaks theologically and contextualizes everything through the Bible. And for all his reminders to Henry not to tell anyone he's an angel, Michael repeatedly admits to Julia and Professor Wutheridge (Monty Woolley), a friend of the family, that he is a divine presence. Julia, though, thinks Michael is speaking in metaphor when he says, "My home is in Heaven" and "God is my father and mother." Michael is a stand-in for Nathan himself, using the character to showcase America's worship of material things at the expense of spiritual centers like the church. Nathan's Michael doesn't understand the way humans have organized religion, and reminisces about an Edenic world "Where everything is perfect, [so] naturally there is no need for regulations."

The love triangle between Michael, Henry, and Julia is the central premise of Nathan's book but has a sensual side to it compared to the more romantic—and chaste—dynamic of the film. Henry is far more of a Puritan in the book. He and Julia are trapped in a loveless, unhappy marriage, with neither interested in divorce because they believe it's their duty to stay together. Henry even writes an op-ed in the paper saying that adultery is the only true grounds for a divorce.

Julia spends her days with her four-year-old daughter Juliet—named after Shakespeare's tragic heroine—whom she watches with fascination because the child is free with her affection, and not tainted by the world's judgmental influences. Julia yearns for an idealized, perfect love and is surprised at the desire—both spiritual and sexual—that Michael inspires within her. As Michael and Julia spend more time together, he starts to notice himself having mortal feelings for her. As Professor Wutheridge reminds him, "You are Immortal, a spirit, a child of light, a pure and perfect being. How can you feel a mortal hunger? . . . Do not mistake this emotion for love." Knowing he can never offer Julia what she wants, Michael leaves without saying goodbye to anyone.

The novel concludes bittersweetly, with Julia and Henry going back to how they were. Julia hopes to have another child as a vessel for her love. Nathan uses this to point out how common relationships like this were at the time. The film, thankfully, gives its characters a happily ever after, with Henry realizing his family is the most important thing to him, reuniting with and devoting himself to Julia, while Dudley watches on, content that he's done his job.

The movie struggled to find an audience upon release, with many assuming the title implied a religious film. Goldwyn retitled the movie *Cary and the Bishop's Wife* in some places, while in others the title became the prominently placed tagline: "Have you heard about Cary and the Bishop's Wife?"

Nathan's work continued to be adapted, most famously the 1948 Jennifer Jones and Joseph Cotten romance *Portrait of Jennie*. *The Bishop's Wife* also served as the inspiration for the television series *Highway to Heaven*, which ran from 1984 to 1989. In 1996, director Penny Marshall remade the movie as *The Preacher's Wife* with Denzel Washington as Dudley, Whitney Houston as Julia, and Courtney B. Vance as Henry.

THE GHOST AND MRS. MUIR

1947

Directed by Joseph L. Mankiewicz
Screenplay by Philip Dunne
Based on *The Ghost and Mrs. Muir* by R. A. Dick, 1945

"You come of age very quickly through shipwreck and disaster."

Lucy Muir (Gene Tierney) is a young widow looking for a new home for herself and her daughter, Anna (Natalie Wood). She buys the quaint Gull Cottage in Whitecliffe-by-the-Sea, but upon entering the house Lucy discovers one little problem: It's haunted. Haunted, specifically, by the ghost of seaman Captain Daniel Gregg (Rex Harrison). Lucy finds the idea of living in a haunted house "fascinating," but Daniel sees her as nothing but a nuisance. He allows her to stay in the home on a trial basis while the pair write Daniel's memoirs, with Lucy acting as a literal ghostwriter. Love soon blossoms between them but is complicated by the fact that while Lucy may act like an angel, Daniel literally resides in Heaven. How will they make it work when "till death do us part" has already happened?

Publishing under the pen name R. A. Dick, author Josephine Leslie wrote just three books in her entire career and the other two weren't as famous as her debut, *The Ghost and Mrs. Muir.* The novel hit shelves right as the United States ended World War II. Little is known about Leslie's life aside from her being Irish and that she settled on the initials R. A. as a tribute to her own sea captain father, Robert Abercromby. (Her heroine's last name pays tribute to him as well, with *muir* being a Gaelic word for the sea.)

Set in the present day, the book reflects a world where women who held down jobs, both at home and abroad during the war, were now being sent back to their domestic lives. Lucy wants to find something to do with her time, like a job, while her family is content to see her either remain a widow, mourning forever, or remarry. As much as Lucy wishes to rebel and tell them what she really wants, she can't. The film changes the time period to the Victorian era to make Lucy's decision to move out of her sister-in-law's home more unorthodox and the pressure to marry more paramount. That, coupled with Lucy's earnest interest in the supernatural, sets her up as eccentric and open to believing in, and falling in love with, Captain Gregg.

Lucy is routinely underestimated and belittled by everyone in her orbit. Introduced to the reader as a "little woman," Lucy is referred to by friends, family, and acquaintances at various points as "little Mrs. Muir," "dear little Mrs. Muir," or "poor little Mrs. Muir." Her family and friends regularly give her unsolicited advice or demand she live life a certain way. Even her son, Cyril, who only exists in the book, chastises her for her choices. Lucy especially butts heads with her sister-in-law Eva, who has a close relationship with Cyril, so much so that she wants to raise him as her own. "All I want is to be left alone to live my life as I wish and not as other people think best for themselves," Lucy says.

Dick's novel is less a conventional romance and more a story of feminine independence. Lucy questions her life choices and feels guilty about how she's raising her children. She even questions whether she loves them enough. Her former marriage is also an opportunity for introspection. She admits she doesn't regret marrying her deceased husband Edwin, but she wasn't happy with him.

She wants to finally fulfill her own desires and, while she worries it's selfish of her to pursue a relationship at all, she falls in love with Miles Fairley (George Sanders). Sanders plays the character terrifically in the movie—charming, smarmy, and suspicious. But he's far more frightening in Dick's book. Miles becomes obsessed with Lucy, so much so that he demands she leave her children with Eva to be with him. "I want you to forget the existence of everyone but me," he says. As in the film, Lucy discovers Miles is actually already married, but in the book Lucy meets his kind wife, as well as another of his mistresses.

The relationship between Lucy and Captain Gregg is present in the novel, though differently. Film historian Jeanine Basinger describes the character on screen as a strong, able man who won't die, a reassuring presence for Lucy. "He is more or less her 'male' side, or that part of her that is brave and independent, fierce and creative." This symbolism is more overt in the book, where the argument can be made that Gregg isn't haunting Lucy at all but is a manifestation of her inner voice that she uses to justify her actions; her conscience transformed into a confident man who tells her what she already knows.

Gregg's dubbing Lucy as "Lucia," a name he says is fit for a queen like her, is a key moment in the movie. It shows Gregg's love and respect for her, his tough outer exterior finally breaking down for her. In the book he calls her Lucia to denote her newfound strength and confidence in a moment when Lucy finally tells off Eva.

Knowing that they can't currently be together, Gregg enchants Lucy to forget him and compels her to move on and live a full life in the movie. It ends with Lucy, now an old woman, sitting down in a chair. The camera shows Captain Gregg, who beckons Lucy to get up, and then turns to show Lucy standing up, looking as she did when she was young. She stands before him and the pair enter an ethereal mist to the next journey of their lives, together for eternity. To the viewer, her walk into the mist with Captain Gregg isn't just a happily ever after, but an awareness that love is eternal and goodbye is never forever. The novel ends similarly, but the final lines see Lucy dying with her head facing the portrait of Gregg. The reader is left with nothing definitive as to whether Gregg was really haunting Lucy or not. They can choose to believe Captain Gregg was real, or a figment of her imagination. No matter what, Lucy's death comes as the result of a life well lived, a life that in some way *was* influenced by Gregg's presence by making her the confident woman she was always meant to be.

A PLACE IN THE SUN

1951

Directed by George Stevens
Screenplay by Michael Wilson and Harry Brown
Based on *An American Tragedy* by Theodore Dreiser, 1925

"Tell mama . . . tell mama all."

A couple goes on what should be a romantic boat trip on an isolated lake. The idyll is shattered when the young, pregnant woman in the boat drowns and the man makes it back to shore. This is the crime at the heart of George Stevens's feature *A Place in the Sun*. An adaptation of Theodore Dreiser's novel *An American Tragedy*, the story follows George Eastman (Montgomery Clift), a working stiff trying to find his place in the world. Leaning on his wealthy uncle for employment, George gets a job at the family factory. Despite a rule prohibiting fraternization between employees, George starts spending time with factory worker Alice Tripp (Shelley Winters). But when George meets and falls for the high-born Angela Vickers (Elizabeth Taylor), Alice starts to cramp his style and becomes even more of a nuisance to him once she reveals to George that she's pregnant with his child.

Today, the glossy, star-studded *A Place in the Sun* is the de facto adaptation of Dreiser's book, but it was actually the second attempt to corral the prodigious novel for the screen. A film version was made in 1931 and released under the book's title, *An American Tragedy*, with Phillips Holmes as Clyde Griffiths (the George Eastman character), Sylvia Sidney as the doomed Roberta Alden (Winters's character), and Frances Dee as the wealthy Sondra Finchley (Taylor's role). Possessing slightly more of Dreiser's story beats than the 1951 version, this adaptation was a critical and commercial disappointment upon release. It didn't help matters that Dreiser absolutely loathed it. Paramount was reluctant to remake the film after that, and the rise of anticommunist sentiment that would define the 1950s made studio execs fear Dreiser's anti-capitalist story might put them under scrutiny.

It's doubtful the Hollywood of the era would have even wanted to adapt Dreiser's novel faithfully. Not only is it over eight hundred pages, but Dreiser's connection to the Naturalism movement—a nineteenth-century literary movement focused on determinism, detachment, scientific objectivism, and social commentary—means his work takes some getting used to. Naturalist writers situate their protagonists as puppets to their genes or their environment. Dreiser took from real life, basing *American Tragedy* on the high-profile 1900s case of Chester Gillette and Grace Brown. As with the movie, Gillette drowned Brown in a lake, allegedly to be with another woman and rid himself of Brown and his unborn child.

In an interview with the American Film Institute (AFI), Stevens said he wanted to make the movie because "I was interested in the mood and emotional effect of the story. I wanted to relate the audience to a character whose behavior it might not subscribe to. To bring that about, one must let the audience see his desire. They have to know his need for the thing that—even accidentally—traps him." Stevens told the studio he'd divorce his movie from the 1931 version by sticking to the book—which he didn't do 100 percent—and renaming all the characters. (George Eastman was conjured up as a combination of Stevens's own name and one half of the Eastman-Kodak partnership.) The studio also retitled the film *A Place in the Sun* to limit claims that the movie was commenting directly on America.

In the book, Clyde is a pathetic character whose life is a series of suffering accidents that he never learns from. He goes through a variety of jobs, from soda jerk to newsboy, before eventually becoming a hotel bellhop, where he's lured into the hedonistic world of material possessions, liquor, and sex. Clyde is written as a selfish teenage boy—just sixteen years old when the book begins—more content to engage in drinking and sex than caring for anyone else. He tries to move away from his fundamentalist upbringing and his relationship with his family. He has a sister named Esta, who is never mentioned or seen in the movie, who meets a traveling actor. The actor seduces Esta and she runs away with him. Clyde has little interest in his sister's problems. When Esta ends up pregnant and abandoned, directly paralleling Roberta and Clyde's relationship, instead of helping her, Clyde spends his money on Hortense Briggs, a girl he's seeing who manipulates him to buy her expensive gifts in exchange for sexual favors. During a night of debauchery Clyde, Hortense, and some friends strike and kill a young girl with their car. Dreiser is a huge fan of foreshadowing—almost too

much so—and this first death sees Clyde flee town rather than deal with the consequences, setting the stage for his eventual plan to do away with Roberta.

Elizabeth Taylor and Montgomery Clift's immense chemistry together—the pair had already shown they were destined to be stars—became a popular selling point for the movie, with posters putting both actors front and center. Their images, often in an embrace or kiss, were used heavily in marketing materials, and that's complemented on-screen where the camera comes in tight on their intimate kisses. Where Alice and George's relationship is implied to be based on lust—a scene of the pair talking in hushed tones inside Alice's house while the camera sits outside feels like a love scene—George and Angela have a more romantic underpinning. Yet the relationship doesn't start to develop until halfway through Dreiser's hundred-chapter book, compared to within the first half of the film.

The character of Sondra Finchley (i.e., the film's Angela Vickers) is as shallow as Clyde. She initially takes an interest in him purely to irritate Clyde's cousin Gilbert Griffiths. She dreams of running away with Clyde, but her devotion to her social standing sees her cast that idea aside. It is the desire to keep Sondra in the lifestyle and social circle she's grown accustomed to that pushes Clyde to murder Roberta.

Both film and novel build to Clyde/George's execution, but their respective changes tweak the overall meaning of their individual stories. In the book, Sondra leaves town to avoid being named in Clyde's high-profile trial. She erases any association with him. She eventually writes him an anonymous letter to say goodbye, shattering Clyde's final dream of a life of wealth and taste with her. A *Place in the Sun* ends on a beautiful romantic sequence in which Angela comes to the jail to visit George one final time. George tells Angela to love him for as long as he has left. The book concludes with Clyde's quest for money and social standing doomed to end in death from the first page, but the movie bittersweetly tears the tragic lovers apart. Clyde committed murder for material gain. George did it for love.

A Place in the Sun would go on to enter the canon of seminal classic films. Charlie Chaplin, upon seeing the movie, called it "the greatest movie ever made about America" and he's not wrong. The movie is a breathtaking exploration of the American dream and man's ability to commit dark deeds in the name of happiness, all set against the horrors of World War II. Dreiser's novel does something similar, though for audiences of the roaring twenties. Nominated for nine Academy Awards, it went on to win six, including Best Screenplay and George Stevens for Best Director.

MY COUSIN RACHEL

1952

Directed by Henry Koster
Screenplay by Nunnally Johnson
Based on *My Cousin Rachel* by Daphne Du Maurier, 1951

"Rachel, my torment. My blessed, blessed torment."

In 1938, British novelist Daphne du Maurier published her novel *Rebecca*. The story of a woman haunted by the spirit of her new husband's first wife, it blends du Maurier's interest in relationships and the paranormal. This theme carried over into her last bestseller, 1951's *My Cousin Rachel*, which follows young Philip Ashley (played in the movie by Richard Burton), who has been raised by his older cousin Ambrose (John Sutton). The two have an incredibly close bond that is strained when Ambrose goes on a trip for his health and, via a letter to Philip, announces that he's married his cousin Rachel (Olivia de Havilland). But when Ambrose dies and Cousin Rachel comes to visit Philip, the younger man is curious about the circumstances of his cousin's death and cannot help falling in love with the beautiful woman. However, is it possible Cousin Rachel had something to do with Ambrose's death? And might Philip be next?

Du Maurier didn't appreciate being considered a romantic author. She situated herself alongside the likes of *Woman in White* author Wilkie Collins, with both having a penchant for unhappy or ambiguous endings and playing with supernatural themes. Critic Kate Kellaway wrote in a 2007 article that "Du Maurier was mistress of calculated irresolution. She did not want to put her readers' minds at rest. She wanted her riddles to persist," and that is certainly the case with the puzzling *My Cousin Rachel*, a book less about romance and more about jealousy and mistrust in a romantic relationship.

Du Maurier became an author ripe for film adaptations, starting with 1939's *Jamaica Inn*, adapted by Alfred Hitchcock. Hitchcock helmed additional Du Maurier adaptations including the aforementioned *Rebecca* in 1940 and *The Birds* in 1963. *My Cousin Rachel* was du Maurier's last bestseller, but she would continue writing and publishing works for another twenty years before her death in 1989. *My Cousin Rachel* was attempted again in 2017, in a version that tries to get closer to Du Maurier's sense of the Gothic and ambiguous. Directed by Roger Michell, the movie stars Rachel Weisz as Rachel and Sam Claflin as Philip.

As with *Rebecca*, a ghost looms over the central relationship between Philip and Rachel. Ambrose's increasingly fraught and paranoid letters, which Philip is sent and finds along the way, are the only glimpses anyone—including Philip himself—gets of the older man's mental state. This paranoia causes Philip to second-guess everything. When Rachel finally arrives in Cornwall to visit Philip, it is Ambrose's portrait that hangs over the room where she sleeps, and a headstone for him, placed at the top of the hill, acts like a dark beacon watching over everything.

Ambrose and Philip become near doubles of themselves, with their relationship containing a heavy amount of queer coding. "I never wanted anyone but Ambrose," Philip says. Our narrator, Philip, is seen by the reader as a headstrong, childish boy despite his age of twenty-four. He and Ambrose live in a manly utopia with no women after Philip loses his mother as an infant and Ambrose fires any nurse who dares to punish the little boy. Philip absolutely refuses to get married but, considering Rachel is Ambrose's wife, the reader understands exactly why he would be open to it. Not only does he fill the literal role of groom—Ambrose's place for Rachel—but it continues the incestuous nature of their relationship as Ambrose and Philip share the same woman.

The film eliminates much of this subtext to pursue a path akin to a Gothic mystery romance. Philip falls in love with Rachel, yes, but is it possible she murdered Ambrose and is plotting Philip's demise as well? For every moment in the film when Rachel shows she isn't interested in Philip's money—returning the family jewels, for instance—the script gives another reason for her to be a murderer, such as having a possible Italian lover, Rainaldi, come to visit. Not only does Rainaldi inflame Philip's jealousy, but for the reader/audience, he might be a coconspirator for Rachel's plot.

This doubling continues with Rachel as well. She is officially Mrs. Ashley, but as Philip falls deeper in love with her, his expectation is that she will become *his* Mrs. Ashley, transferring ownership of her title from one man to the other.

Director Henry Koster and screenwriter Nunnally Johnson craft *My Cousin Rachel* in the style of *Rebecca* or *Dragonwyck*, but Du Maurier writes a story about the way women of the 1830s were controlled through marriage. Finances play a heavy hand, with Ambrose's fervid letters about Rachel's spending habits looking like the ravings of a man desperate to keep every penny for himself. Philip appears to benevolently transfer all his wealth to Rachel, but he's aware that according to the customs of the period, Rachel's remarriage sees her money controlled by her husband, who in this case is Philip. Philip's intentions could be equally nefarious and selfish. The question of the book is who is truly poisoning whom, as Rachel appears to become a prisoner in Philip's house and starts to look progressively weary as things go on. But because Philip is the gaze through which the reader sees everything, there's always a tint of ambiguity.

My Cousin Rachel was a big deal for De Havilland, as she had walked away from Hollywood after winning the Oscar for *The Heiress* (1949) and welcomed the birth of her first child. De Havilland commands the screen as Rachel, playing a character who has to be sweet but also give the viewer enough to believe that she could, in theory, be a villain. (Chemistry was a struggle on the set, with Burton saying later that De Havilland came off as snooty and demanded that everyone refer to her as "Ms. De Havilland.")

Rachel's eventual demise—falling through an unrepaired footbridge to the rocks below—has a different meaning between the film and book. The film ends with Rachel asking Philip, "Why?" Why didn't he warn her that the footbridge was broken and, a question unspoken, why didn't he trust her? Rachel becomes his "torment," as Philip struggles with the guilt of not believing she was an honest woman. Du Maurier ends her novel with it still unclear what Rachel's true intentions were, because our unreliable narrator is never able to figure them out himself. Was Rachel ever a villain? Was she at one point, and then she truly fell in love with Philip? Did she kill

Ambrose, or was the brain tumor he was diagnosed with at fault? The reader is never meant to know, though the movie seems to imply that Rachel was innocent. Regardless, Rachel is only able to say the word "Ambrose" before she dies in the book. In this final moment, Ambrose and Philip are again confused with each other and doomed to be one and the same for eternity. The love story at the heart of both versions is of one man's love for a woman and how that's ultimately overpowered by his own love for his cousin and, by extension, himself.

A FAREWELL TO ARMS

1957

Directed by Charles Vidor
Screenplay by Ben Hecht
Based on *A Farewell to Arms*
by Ernest Hemingway, 1929

"When you love you wish to do things for. You wish to sacrifice for. You wish to serve."

Ernest Hemingway's wartime novel *A Farewell to Arms* is considered one of the most heart-wrenching love stories ever written, as well as a stark, brutal portrait of the horrors Hemingway and others endured during World War I. The author drew inspiration for *A Farewell to Arms* from an incident that took place on July 8, 1918, when a trench mortar shell struck him. Hemingway was sent to a Milan hospital, where he met and fell in love with Red Cross nurse Agnes von Kurowsky.

History has disputed much of Hemingway's story—many say he certainly embellished the details of the accident—but either way, it compelled him to write the story of an American ambulance driver in Italy, Frederick Henry, as he tries to make it out of the Great War alive, and his relationship with nurse Catherine Barkley.

Hemingway eschews florid prose to tell the story bluntly, declaratively. This style was far from the norm in the 1920s and 1930s compared to the more baroque stylings of books at the time, influenced more by the Victorian era than anything modern. Hemingway recounts the story like a journalist, with a detached, emotionless tone, to put the reader in Henry's mindset. Henry has no connection to the war. He doesn't fight for a cause and, in one scene from the book, encourages a fellow soldier to throw away a truss belt for his hernia so the soldier can go to the hospital.

War is omnipresent in the novel, so the characters try hard to think about and do anything that will distract them. The book is filled with sections where characters have conversations, make fun of each other, and otherwise try to ignore the war-torn landscape around them. That includes wantonly engaging in love. Catherine and Henry's love story isn't necessarily a timeless tale of boy meets girl but, as Hemingway depicts it, the story of two people pretending to love and care for each other to overcome their own fears, pain, and grief that the war has brought them.

Hemingway's work was routinely adapted for film, and *A Farewell to Arms* was the first to be translated to the big screen with the 1932 feature directed by Frank Borzage starring Gary Cooper as Henry and Helen Hayes as Catherine. Hemingway didn't care for the movie, an unsurprising response to most of the films based on his works. Producer David O. Selznick, after a four-year hiatus from filmmaking, wanted to take another stab at the feature but didn't have the rights, which were held by Warner Bros. In a bit of studio horse trading, Warner Bros. sought the foreign rights to *A Star Is Born* (1954), which just

so happened to be in Selznick's hands and allowed for each studio to get the movies they wanted.

Selznick cast Rock Hudson—the hottest star of the 1950s—as Frederick Henry. Hudson jumped on the opportunity, turning down roles in *The Bridge on the River Kwai* (1957) and *Ben-Hur* (1959) to play the character. As nurse Catherine Barkley there was only one person Selznick wanted: his wife, actress Jennifer Jones. Jones's casting is one of the biggest divergences from the source material. Not only was she thirty-eight years old at the time, playing the twenty-one-year-old Catherine, but one of the first things Henry is struck by upon meeting Catherine in the book is her long blonde hair. Jones's hair is raven black in the film.

Filmed on location in Italy as well as at the famed Cinecittà Studios in Rome, the movie is beautifully shot, even if it removes much of Hemingway's source material. Because of the author's apathetic exploration of war and the long stretches of violence, coupled with moments of random interaction that take place in the slim tome, the movie plays up the relationship between Catherine and Henry. There are moments when the movie showcases the playacting of the pair's romance, with Catherine smiling wide and telling Henry, "Keep right on lying to me. That's what I want you to do." It's one of the few acknowledgments of Hemingway's point: that Catherine and Frederick don't necessarily have a love for the ages but are lying about their affection for each other to escape the war. Henry also spends a significant amount of time in the book drunk or drinking, an easy nix for the film, which positions Frederick Henry as a charming soldier, not an apathetic drunk.

However, the movie heavily implies Henry and Catherine's illicit romance and sexual encounters. Hemingway doesn't go into detail on Catherine and Henry's sexual encounters because he expects the reader to read between the lines. One scene in the movie sees Catherine look into the hospital hallway as Henry calls to her and she slowly closes the door. This is how the pair's first sexual encounter is detailed in the book. Hemingway subscribed to what he called the iceberg theory of writing: "If a writer of prose knows enough about what he is writing about he may omit things that he knows and the reader, if the writer is writing truly enough, will have a feeling of those things as strongly as though the writer had stated them. The dignity of movement of an ice-berg is due to only one-eighth of it being above water." (The book was still charged with indecency upon publication in 1929.) Though the novel and movie end tragically, the audience watches Catherine and Henry revel in being in love and unmarried. Catherine even says in both versions that "I couldn't be any more married" to Henry.

Because the novel is Henry's story, Hemingway plays on

another prominent theme found in his writing: the fraternity of men. The men share a love for wine, women, and boldness on the battlefield. Their personalities shine as they spend their days jokingly ribbing a local priest for his celibacy. In the movie, this theme manifests through the character of Rinaldi (Vittorio De Sica, in an Oscar-nominated performance). Rinaldi is one of Henry's closest friends and they spend much of the novel carousing and trying to ignore the war together. Rinaldi's character is combined in the movie with another random soldier, who is captured alongside Henry by the battle police for interrogation. Rinaldi slowly fades from the book's narrative as Henry flees into Switzerland with Catherine. Henry spends time wondering what happened to him. In the film, Rinaldi embraces nihilism, which causes the police to believe he is a German infiltrator and execute him. It's a fantastic performance by De Sica, who makes you care for this gregarious character who becomes hollowed out by the war, even if he doesn't exist in the source material.

Hemingway was said to have written thirty-nine different drafts for the book's ending (some sources say forty-seven). The movie presents a glossy and sumptuous love story for the preceding two hours, but it still retains Hemingway's dour conclusion: Catherine, pregnant with Henry's child, dies during childbirth alongside the baby. Henry, losing the love of his life and child, walks aimlessly in the rain.

This ending was a departure from the 1932 version, which was said to have had a happy ending filmed alongside one more reminiscent of the book (though ambiguous). Catherine's death is one of the most tragic deaths in literature because it is the final shattering of Frederick's dreams and proof that, for all their best efforts, the war has touched them. It hurts all the more for what it doesn't give the reader: catharsis. Catherine's death doesn't bring a grand revelation to Henry nor does anything change because of it. The war still goes on. Anything like that would be perceived as false in Hemingway's hyper-realistic purview.

The movie had a very contentious shoot, with original director John Huston leaving the project after repeated clashes with Selznick. As screenwriter Ben Hecht described it, "It was the case of two Caesars and one Alp." Released just three months after another Hemingway adaptation, *The Sun Also Rises* (1957), *A Farewell to Arms* was a flop upon release and ended the once great David O. Selznick's producing career. Sam Goldwyn said it best when trying to discourage Selznick from remaking it: "It's a mistake to remake a great picture because you can never make it better." No matter what, it was a launch-pad for viewers to go back and read Hemingway's incomparable tale of love during wartime.

BREAKFAST AT TIFFANY'S

1961

Directed by Blake Edwards
Screenplay by George Axelrod
Based on *Breakfast at Tiffany's* by Truman Capote, 1958

"People don't belong to people."

The empty streets of New York City. A woman dressed in a floor-length black dress with a tiara atop her head gets out of a cab. As Henry Mancini's "Moon River" plays, she walks in front of a store, pulls a pastry and cup of coffee out of a bag, and gazes at the diamonds in the front window of the jewelry store Tiffany's. This opening scene to Blake Edwards's *Breakfast at Tiffany's* is an indelible moment in film history. Since its release in 1961, *Breakfast at Tiffany's* has become an aspirational and aesthetic touchpoint for its fans, with replicas of Audrey Hepburn's Givenchy-designed gowns and sunglasses easily available.

The film follows Hepburn's Holly Golightly, a New York socialite who fills her days going on dates with various rich men. When things go wrong, she returns to Tiffany's, the one place where she can relax. After writer Paul Varjak (George Peppard) moves into Holly's apartment building, the two become kindred spirits; she is dating men for their money and Paul is the kept man of a woman he refers to only as "2E" (Patricia Neal). Paul tries to grow closer to Holly, but her belief that "people don't belong to people" and that she'll only marry for money threatens their budding relationship.

Breakfast at Tiffany's is so inseparable from Hepburn's performance that many forget the film is based on Truman Capote's 1958 novella of the same name. Perhaps that is due to screenwriter George Axelrod and director Blake Edwards seeing the story as a romantic comedy, whereas Capote crafts a character study.

Set in the 1940s, Capote's unnamed male narrator finds Holly to be a curious object but isn't romantically interested in her, with the allusion that he is gay (and a surrogate for Capote himself). The narrator arrives in New York City in hopes of making his way as a writer. He is not established like Paul in the movie. The narrator, a bartender named Joe Bell—to whom the narrator recounts his memories of Holly to in the first place—and Holly's former paramour, Rusty Trawler, all have gay overtones in the novella. (Not to mention Holly, who says in response to people thinking she's a lesbian, "Of course I am. Everyone is: a bit. So what?")

Capote was inspired by several different women when he wrote Holly Golightly, including Walter Matthau's wife Carol Grace, writer Doris Lilly, Oona Chaplin, Gloria Vanderbilt, and Capote's own mother, Lillie Mae Faulk. He also had a clear picture of who he wanted to play Holly in the film: actress Marilyn Monroe. Capote, who wrote Holly clearly as a sex worker, felt Marilyn had an earthier quality to her compared to the sophisticated and gamine Hepburn. "Holly Golightly was . . . a tough character, not an Audrey Hepburn type at all." Different stories over the years have said Monroe tried hard to get the role, while others say she passed on the character to work with her husband Arthur Miller on *The Misfits* (1961). Kim Novak and Shirley MacLaine were also considered.

Capote's Holly Golightly is a woman of questionable morals with no direction in life.

As Capote himself said, "The main reason I wrote about Holly . . . was that she was such a symbol of all these girls who come to New York and spin in the sun for a moment . . . and then disappear. I wanted to rescue one girl from that anonymity and preserve her for posterity." Axelrod's script makes Holly and Paul similar in that both have dubious romantic relationships—because of the studio era, Holly and Paul are never overtly labeled as sex workers—to further their own aims.

Holly eventually disappears for good in the book after becoming pregnant by José (José Luis de Vilallonga), the boyfriend of her friend Mag. She plans to marry him and move to Brazil, but after she's arrested for her connection to a drug ring run by gangster Sally Tomato, Holly ends up in the hospital and loses the baby. She's determined to flee the country and head to Brazil, which she ultimately does.

Unlike the movie, in which Paul, Holly, and her pet cat, Cat, reunite to form a makeshift family, Holly goes to Brazil and the narrator never hears from her again, apart from a single letter with no return address. The narrator says if Holly ever reached out, he'd tell her that her cat, which she abandoned on the sidewalk, eventually found a good home and that he hopes Holly did as well. The movie has a happily ever after for its characters, but Capote ends Holly's story with only the hope that she found happiness on her own terms, though the reader will never know for sure.

Blake Edwards gave us a love story about two adrift characters who engaged in easy sex, by trade, before finding true love and living happily ever after. Truman Capote told a story about a lonely man living life through the eyes of a fascinating woman he never forgot.

Breakfast at Tiffany's entered the pop culture canon and was a smash hit upon release. The movie was nominated for five Academy Awards, including one for Hepburn, though the film only won two: for Henry Mancini's score and his song "Moon River," itself now a staple outside of the movie. Holly sings a song in the novella, but its lyrics are darker: "Don't wanna sleep. Don't wanna die. Just wanna go a-travelin' through the pastures of the sky," implying her desire for freedom. For Mancini, "Moon River" wouldn't have existed without Hepburn, specifically, playing Holly. "It's unique for a composer to really be inspired by a person, a face or a personality, but Audrey certainly inspires me."

Because Capote's work is a novella, Axelrod and Edwards were forced to expand the story, with many of the changes being for "audience approval," as Edwards said. One character that is expanded upon, unfortunately, is Mr. Yunioshi (Mickey Rooney), Holly's exasperated Japanese landlord. The film's racist depiction of the character, with Rooney in buck teeth and slanted eyes speaking in a faux-Japanese dialect, is a tragic slight against the movie. In later years, both Edwards and producer Richard Shepherd admitted that they regretted including the character.

DOCTOR ZHIVAGO

1965

Directed by David Lean
Screenplay by Robert Bolt
Based on *Doctor Zhivago* by Boris Pasternak, 1957

"Wouldn't it have been lovely if we'd met before?"

David Lean's adaptation of *Doctor Zhivago* is as grand and sweeping as the Boris Pasternak book on which it's based. Lean, the man behind *Lawrence of Arabia* (1962) and *The Bridge on the River Kwai*, sought to return to the world of intimate, romantic movies like his 1945 romance *Brief Encounter*, which, like Pasternak's characters, sees its lovers torn between duty to a spouse and their own personal desires. When the opportunity came for Lean to adapt Pasternak's over five-hundred-page novel, he jumped at it.

Both book and film detail the Russian Revolution of 1917 and its aftermath through the eyes of Doctor Yuri Zhivago (Omar Sharif), and focus on his love triangle with his wife Tonya (Geraldine Chaplin) and his mistress Lara (Julie Christie).

The lead-up to the publication of *Doctor Zhivago* in 1957 is worthy of its own movie. Pasternak was the child of a Jewish artist and concert pianist. His family was enmeshed in Russia's artistic circles. Fellow Russian authors Leo Tolstoy and Rainer Maria Rilke were friends. Similar to Zhivago himself, Pasternak studied music before switching to philosophy. He eventually gave that up to settle as a poet in 1913. That was just the beginning of utilizing his own life for *Doctor Zhivago*. Much of the book was inspired by Pasternak's experiences during the Russian Revolution and his affair with a woman named Olga Ivinskaya, who served as the basis for Lara.

Doctor Zhivago was banned in the USSR, cited for being a novel that showed the "hatred of socialism." So it was smuggled out of the country and originally published in Italy in 1957 before debuting in the United States in 1958. The book's international success, sadly, didn't help Pasternak. After he was awarded the Nobel Prize for Literature in 1958, he was forced to refuse it by the Russian government. Russian critics called him a traitor and a libeler. Pasternak was expelled from the Union of Soviet Writers, and though he and Ivinskaya were no longer together, she was arrested. Pasternak lived in exile just outside of Moscow in an artists' colony until his death from lung cancer in 1960.

Because of Lean's direction and the novel's acclaim, the roles were highly sought after by Hollywood's stars. Producer Carlo Ponti wanted to adapt the novel for his wife, actress Sophia Loren, which Lean immediately shot down. He cited to Ponti that Loren was too tall for the character, but it's said it was more because Lean didn't see her as able to play a virgin.

Audrey Hepburn was briefly considered for the role of Tonya before Chaplin's casting. And while Sharif is now synonymous with the character, Lean originally wanted his *Lawrence of Arabia* star Peter O'Toole in the role. Sharif originally wanted to play the idealistic Pasha (who was ultimately portrayed by Tom Courtenay), who later rebrands himself as the revolutionary leader Strelnikov.

There was no possibility that Lean could adapt the entirety of Pasternak's novel, even with the finished product coming in at nearly three and a half hours long. To help anchor audiences, the movie starts with the introduction of Yuri's half-brother Yevgraf (Alec Guinness), a character invented for the film, attempting to find Lara and Yuri's daughter. He locates a woman who could be her and proceeds to tell the girl the story of her parentage. The novel starts at the beginning of Yuri's life, with the death of his mother. (Though his name is "Yury" in the novel, I'll continue to refer to him by the spelling used for him in the movie.) The reveal of Yuri and Lara's daughter happens by chance toward the end of the book, when Yuri's old friends Misha and Nicky meet her while fighting in World War II.

Because the movie adapts about half of the book, it loses much of the political background and motivation for the characters. This technique is found in other adaptations of literary epics, like *Anna Karenina*. The Revolution in the movie doesn't give the viewer background on the why behind the fighting, short of the working people struggling for freedom. Critics complained at the time of the film's release that, by focusing exclusively on Yuri's relationship with Lara, it romanticized the bloody revolution.

Other changes were the result of needing to keep the character count manageable—always a problem with Russian literature—and move the story along as swiftly as possible. Yuri goes to live with his uncle Kolya in the book, who becomes a famous writer and moves to Switzerland. Once Yuri is in medical school, he meets Tonya and the two marry. In the film, Uncle Kolya becomes Alexander (Ralph Richardson), Tonya's father, and Tonya and Yuri know each other from childhood. Their marriage is more the result of their close, familial bond. And while Yuri reserves his deepest love for Lara, he goes to Moscow and starts living with a woman named Marina, with whom he falls in love and has two children. Yuri's decision to choose between Tonya and Marina becomes a key choice in the novel's third act.

Yuri is a frustrating character on the page, lacking much of the action and romanticism found in Omar Sharif's performance, which, shockingly enough, was not one of the film's ten Oscar nominations. When Yuri is held captive by the army and decides to leave, he does so by simply walking away. Compare the same moment in the movie, when Sharif's Yuri makes the decision and gallops away on horseback through the snowy landscape—a far more kinetic image. Yuri is more firmly a hero, a man of the action in the film, compared to the more sensitive, interior poet in the novel. The novel makes a point of ending with an anthology of Yuri's poems to showcase his literary fortitude, which couldn't translate to film.

Doctor Zhivago was the first Western film to show the Russian Revolution. It tied with *The Sound of Music* (1965) for the most Oscars during the 1966 Academy Awards, winning five, in addition to ushering in other Russian and Soviet-era historical epics like *Nicholas and Alexandra* (1971) and *Reds* (1981).

PIERROT LE FOU

1965

Directed by Jean-Luc Godard
Screenplay by Jean-Luc Godard
Based on *Obsession* by Lionel White, 1963

"Film is like a battleground. There's love, hate, action, violence, death . . . in one word: emotion."

There's a moment in Jean-Luc Godard's *Pierrot le fou* when the protagonist Ferdinand (Jean-Paul Belmondo) goes to a hip party with his wife. The people speak in commercial slogans, hawking products that, by extension, sell themselves and their worth. Ferdinand meets a successful film director, played by real-life director Samuel Fuller of *The Naked Kiss* fame (1964), who lays out what every good movie needs: emotion expressed through love, hate, action, violence, and death. In the nearly two-hour run time of Godard's film, the audience experiences all of those things wrapped up in a quasi-noir story of love and deceit. Its source material has those things as well, albeit in a vastly different story from what Godard presents on-screen.

Author Lionel White's work had already received the big-screen treatment prior to *Pierrot le fou*. His 1955 story *Clean Break* was translated by Stanley Kubrick into *The Killing* the following year. Godard was drawn to White's 1963 novel *Obsession*, which tells the story of an out-of-work husband and father, Conrad Madden, who gives up his wife and children to run away with seventeen-year-old babysitter Allie after she kills a man. The pair's relationship is strained as their crimes become more frequent, leaving Conrad to discover what he's capable of.

Fascinated by the story of a man who runs off with a younger girl and "gets into a series of adventures," Godard envisioned an English-language feature with his then-wife, Anna Karina, as the Lolita-esque Allie and Richard Burton in the role of Madden. That initial casting wasn't possible, leaving Godard to turn to his former *Breathless* (1960) star Belmondo for the lead role. Unfortunately, casting Belmondo opposite Karina completely changed the tone and dynamic of the story, as only seven years in age separated the two, far from Godard's vision of a May–December romance story along the lines of Jean Renoir's *La chienne* (1931). Godard altered the preexisting script to accommodate the pair by turning Belmondo's Ferdinand and Karina's Marianne into "the last romantic couple," the last couple willing to do whatever they needed to for love and to be together. Taking inspiration from poets like Goethe and the eponymous protagonist of his novel *The Sorrows of Young Werther*, Godard situates the relationship as one where Ferdinand is deeply, obsessively in love with Marianne, while knowing it will always be an unrequited romance.

White's book is a straightforward noir in the vein of *The Postman Always Rings Twice*, wherein the relationship is sexually charged but filled with distrust. It plays with conventions of masculinity and the American dream in that thirty-eight-year-old Conrad, having recently lost his job, and emasculated by his wife and children, is drawn to Allie because of her youth. When the pair are on the run and are forced to take on aliases as a married couple, Conrad takes the opportunity to push Allie into dressing and acting sophisticated to cover up for her age, but it also shows his control of her to make up for the lack of control in his own life. "She looked exactly as I wanted her to look," he says.

He falls into a comfortable existence with the teenager, hiding out in Aiken, South Carolina, and pretending to be a wealthy man. The obsession of the title isn't just Conrad's extreme adoration of Allie, but his obsession with finding control in life. White's book is a noir, so the protagonists in these stories never have control and to try to find it is futile. When Allie kills again and gangster kingpin Ace Blackmer comes searching for them, Conrad believes it is sheer dumb bad luck. As he reiterates time and again, he can't believe Allie is involved or would try to frame him. He believes she loves him as deeply as he does her. His obsession leads to blindness and, as in any good noir, his own downfall.

Godard utilizes the book's opening to a degree, with Belmondo's Ferdinand being in an estranged marriage with his wife, Maria (Graziella Galvani), but from there the director abandons the book completely, with twenty-five-year-old Karina playing Marianne as a woman who was previously in a relationship with Ferdinand, rather than the teenage babysitter. The viewer never knows the details of their past together and, in the grand scheme of things, it's unimportant. Ferdinand and Marianne spend the night together and a dreamlike sequence of events takes place that sees them rekindle their relationship. Ferdinand discovers a corpse in Marianne's apartment and she reveals she's being chased by members of the OAS, a French far-right terrorist organization established during the Algerian War.

Godard uses the basic outline of White's novel and mixes genres like the road movie and comedy to tell a cultural satire of bourgeois apathy and alienation. This makes sense considering the French setting. Ferdinand's life before Allie is one of mindless parties and consumerism, and even once he and Allie strike out on their own, the pair are still isolated because of both their crimes and the world around them.

Throughout the book, Allie talks about her "brother" Joel, though the reader is given every indication that he is actually her lover, a fact copied in the movie. Joel coerces Conrad into one big score: helping him rob the casino where Joel works. Things go sour, and the ensuing story Conrad tells is a confession written after he's murdered Allie and Joel and called the police. Conrad's lone moment of control comes in making the decision to turn himself in.

Ferdinand, however, doesn't get any of that in Godard's film. He kills Marianne and her lover (named Fred in the film) and decides to blow himself up by attaching sticks of dynamite to his head. At the last second Ferdinand changes his mind, but it's too late. Ferdinand's obsession, growing frustration, and eventual violent split with Marianne is, according to some critics, a metaphor for Godard's own deteriorating relationship with Karina. The pair had been together since 1961 and divorced right before production started.

In the end, all the elements Fuller mentioned are present in *Pierrot le fou*, even if they aren't in *Obsession*. For Godard, love can't keep you together and, for all your attempts to try, it's a lost cause—as evidenced by his own real-life marriage. For White, love is about control, a way to fill the void for the lack of individual control.

THE GRADUATE

1967

Directed by Mike Nichols
Screenplay by Calder Willingham and Buck Henry
Based on *The Graduate* by Charles Webb, 1963

"Mrs. Robinson, you're trying to seduce me."

There's no more iconic image than a befuddled Ben Braddock (Dustin Hoffman) staring at the alluring femme fatale Mrs. Robinson (Anne Bancroft), with the camera shooting him from underneath her leg. In his second film after *Who's Afraid of Virginia Woolf* (1966), director Mike Nichols crafts a movie filled to the gills with images that have been parodied throughout popular culture, coupled with a fabulous soundtrack by Simon and Garfunkel. But take away the music and cinematography and *The Graduate* is one of the seminal movies of the 1960s, telling the story of a confused youth seduced—literally and figuratively—and betrayed by a corrupt and decadent older generation.

Hoffman's Benjamin is a college graduate so adrift he spends his days floating in the pool at his parent's house, uninterested in going to graduate school or getting a job. Trying to find some meaning in life, Benjamin embarks on an affair with Mrs. Robinson, the wife of his father's partner. But things become complicated when Benjamin falls for Mrs. Robinson's daughter Elaine (Katharine Ross).

Author Charles Webb borrowed from his own life for his 1963 novel. Born to a wealthy Pasadena surgeon, Webb based much of Benjamin Braddock on himself, and Elaine Robinson on his eventual wife. While it's easy to presume Webb's mother-in-law, Jo Rudd, was the inspiration for Mrs. Robinson, Rudd and Webb disputed this for years. Every studio refused to finance an adaptation of the book because "they read the book and hated it, and no one thought it was funny," said producer Lawrence Turman. It wasn't until producer Joseph E. Levine offered to help finance the movie, and Turman got Nichols to direct, that the movie finally started production.

Since Webb's novel is so dialogue heavy, screenwriters Buck Henry and Calder Willingham adapted Webb's novel verbatim. (One of the few inventions for the film is the famous "plastics" line a family friend says to Ben.) Benjamin is unable to fit into the world of his peers who are going to college or working, nor does he inhabit the world of the adults around him who spend their days drinking and pining for their lost youth. The fact that the adults are only referred to as "Mr." or "Mrs." and that young people, like Ben and Elaine, have actual names shows how deep the gulf is between the two groups.

The book is far more of a black comedy, with the humor deriving from the utter absurdity of the situations Ben finds himself in. As a character, Ben Braddock is a nondescript man so disillusioned and uninterested in life that he can't make a simple decision as to whether he wants a drink, let alone if he wants to go to graduate school—he's accepted into Harvard and Yale in the book—or teach, having won a prestigious scholarship

in his field of study. His father asks him at one point in the book, "Have you just lost all hope?"

Ben's parents, particularly his father (William Daniels in the movie), are far more involved in the book than the self-absorbed showboaters they are in the movie. Ben decries their desire to tout his accomplishments, saying, "I have been a goddamn—a goddamn Ivy-covered status symbol around here for four years," taking his parents by surprise. When Ben wants to travel the world and find "simple honest people that can't even read or write their own name," Ben's father gives him money to do so, though Ben is back home in three weeks and claims there was nothing interesting in the world. When the affair with Mrs. Robinson is revealed and Ben is committed to marrying Elaine at all costs, Ben's father travels to Berkeley to bring Ben home and have him see a psychiatrist, presuming his son is in the midst of a psychotic break. When Ben refuses, his father slaps him, the first real action his father takes in the novel.

The relationship with the alluring and dangerous Mrs. Robinson plays out similarly between book and film, but the reader learns more about the state of her marriage—she and her husband have slept in separate bedrooms for the last five years, and only sleep together when Mr. Robinson is drunk. Otherwise the loneliness and bitterness of the character is the same on-screen. Both book and movie show that love is constantly in conflict, and changing with age. The Robinsons are in a loveless marriage, whereas Ben truly believes Elaine is his soulmate despite their brief courtship. Like the cynicism of trying to find meaning in life, falling in love is just as empty and fleeting, according to Webb.

Nichols found Mrs. Robinson to be an example of "the great American danger we're all in, that we'll bargain away the experience of being alive for the appearance of it." In the book, we learn more about why Mrs. Robinson is so determined to keep Ben and Elaine apart. Much of it is motivated by jealousy of her child, but Mrs. Robinson explains to Ben that Elaine is "a very simple girl. She is sweet and she is uncomplicated . . . she is thoroughly honest . . . she is thoroughly sincere" and "you [Ben] are none of these things." So while the parents in the movie may seem vapid and self-absorbed, the book shows there is a sense of compassion for their children and a desire for them to avoid the past mistakes of the parents. It's just that the adults don't know how to talk to their kids about it.

There's much duality in Ben's life: his two different women (Elaine and Mrs. Robinson), the two California settings (Los Angeles and Berkeley), and Ben's moral drifting and indecisiveness versus his commitment. Ben and Elaine's relationship in the book plays out akin to his relationship with Mrs. Robinson.

But since Elaine is the babe in the woods, Ben takes the role of the coldhearted partner. During his affair with Mrs. Robinson, Ben complains about wanting to talk to her and have their relationship be more than physical. When he and Elaine start dating, she wants to know more about who he is and what he wants in life—important things that definitely need an answer once Ben decides to marry Elaine. Elaine is far more interesting in the confines of the book, with her clarity that the marriage won't work. "Before you tie yourself down to being married you should do other things," she tells Ben.

Ben is resistant to sharing his beliefs with her, since he doesn't have any. He becomes so bored with his life that he arbitrarily reads a book, about which he has nothing to say when Elaine asks him about it. This moment mimics a similar scene in both versions when Ben asks Mrs. Robinson about how she spends her days. She responds with "reading," but can't recall the title of the book.

Ben's desire to marry Elaine turns into outright obsession in the book's third act. Since the filmmakers didn't have the rights to shoot on the Berkeley campus, the movie sees Ben watch Elaine from afar before he jumps on a bus with her to the city zoo. But the book shows him outright stalking the campus looking for her, even sitting outside her dorm. When her father pulls her out of school after the Robinson affair is revealed, Ben goes so far as to stand on a chair in the college cafeteria and interrogate the female residents about whether they know Elaine. He later makes Elaine's roommate, Marjory, call Mrs. Robinson before he grabs the phone out of her hands. Benjamin Braddock is a bit psychotic, to say the least.

It's impossible to think of *The Graduate* ending differently than how it's presented in the movie, with Benjamin barging into Elaine's wedding after she says, "I do," and the two running onto a bus, their laughter turning to quiet contemplation and ambivalence as Simon and Garfunkel's "The Sound of Silence" plays. The basic bones of that ending are Webb's, and the book ends on the same ambivalent tone as the film. After jumping off the balcony and crashing the wedding, Ben eventually stops Elaine as she's walking down the aisle. The two run out of the church and onto the bus looking a bit worse for wear; Ben's shirt is ripped "down to his knees" and Elaine's dress is dragged over cigarette butts on the bus floor. The book's final lines are: "'Benjamin.' 'What.' The bus begins to move."

Ben and Elaine end the movie questioning whether they'll be like their parents. Ben Braddock has just as little direction as he did at the beginning—not knowing where he's going and not particularly caring. But this seemingly unromantic ending has a touch of irony within it. Despite all Ben's waffling on making a decision, he *has* made a series of them, all motivated by his love (or whatever you want to call it) for Elaine. He set out to do something and he accomplished it. Regardless of whether they end up like their parents ten or twenty years in the future, Ben and Elaine made an adult decision to fall in love and see what comes of it.

Author Peter Biskind said the release of *The Graduate* "sent tremors through the industry." It was one of several films to showcase a new way of filmmaking with a focus on social criticism. *The Graduate* was nominated for seven Academy Awards but only won one, for director Mike Nichols. In 2007, author Charles Webb showed readers what happened to Ben and Elaine with the sequel novel *Home School*, which follows a now married Ben and Elaine in the 1970s attempting to homeschool their two sons and dealing with a drop-in from an elderly Mrs. Robinson.

WOMEN IN LOVE

1969

Directed by Ken Russell
Screenplay by Larry Kramer
Based on *Women in Love* by D. H. Lawrence, 1920

"Try to love me a little more and want me a little less."

Author D. H. Lawrence is one of Britain's most provocative authors, whose works challenge the sexual mores of the time. While not as sexually explicit as his 1928 novel *Lady Chatterley's Lover*, his 1920 book *Women in Love* contains much of what made Lawrence such an audacious writer, with its story of sisters Ursula (Jennie Linden) and Gudrun Brangwen (Glenda Jackson) and their respective relationships with best friends Rupert Birkin (Alan Bates) and Gerald Crich (Oliver Reed). Shy schoolteacher Ursula wants love and romance, but is stymied by Rupert's constant cynicism about the world. Gudrun, named after a violent character in Norse literature, is freer, an artist in love with the growing world of bohemia. Gerald, for all his attempts to not live like his coal miner father—Lawrence is said to have based much of Gerald on himself—finds his masculinity threatened by Gudrun's independence.

As directed by Ken Russell in 1969, with a script by playwright and future LGBTQ+ activist Larry Kramer, the movie version of *Women in Love* is less an adaptation of this specific book and more a love letter to Lawrence in general. Kramer said he translated about half of the novel while incorporating passages and other elements from Lawrence's letters, essays, poems, and plays. A specific scene wherein Rupert discusses the proper way to consume a fig, his description loaded with highly erotic imagery, is a direct recitation of Lawrence's 1924 poem "Figs."

While Russell became known as a director prone to weirdness and shock value, the film is a fairly straightforward story of two couples and their differing viewpoints on love, marriage, and romance. It is more of an ensemble piece than the book, with Gudrun's integration into the bohemian art scene and Ursula's attempt to reconcile with her own sexuality, balanced with Gerald's and Birkin's, all present. For Russell and Kramer, the story is about repressed sexuality and how, even if one finds someone they connect with, monogamy and true love are strictly illusory. People will always self-sabotage and wonder about how their life would be without their significant other.

Despite the book's title, Lawrence is more interested in Gerald than any other character, no doubt because Gerald held much in common with the author. An entire chapter is devoted to Gerald's relationship to the mines and his feeling of omnipotence at controlling people's fates through employment.

There is also more description on Gerald's familial history. It's said that he accidentally killed his brother by telling the boy to look down the barrel of an old gun, unaware that it was loaded. Although it's never made clear what Gerald's intentions were, the implication is that it was not an accident but truly Gerald's chronic desire to kill those he loves or is close to.

Gerald's casting in the movie goes against Lawrence's conception of him on the page. Gerald is described as blond and "pure as an arctic thing." There's an air of artificiality in Gerald, enhanced by his glossy blond facade. Yet Reed's casting works because he understands Gerald's wolflike bearing as a character. During the book's final part, his desire for godlike power comes off like madness, as Gerald is determined to kill Gudrun rather than lose her to someone else or be emasculated by her.

The script takes only specific sections of the actual narrative, removing over half the chapters wherein Lawrence philosophizes. It's understandable why Kramer didn't focus heavily on the book, as Lawrence spends entire chapters sermonizing his thoughts on sex as a means of spiritual and literal regeneration with all the fervor of a preacher touting a new religion. His prose is highly florid, punctuated with an extensive use of adjectives. While Lawrence is considered a Modernist writer, his work hearkens back to Romantic-era writers like John Keats. For Lawrence, man is at his best when he's surrounded by nature. Several scenes in the movie and the novel see the characters strip naked to find peace and freedom in the woods. His thoughts on love are that one never truly gives themselves over to another without losing control and freedom.

Lawrence also believes that true emotional connection comes exclusively through a fraternity of men. He writes that "the heart of each [man, Gerald and Birkin] burned from the other. They burned with each other, inwardly. This they will never admit." When Gerald dies at the novel's conclusion, it is Birkin who claims his body and plans to bury him in the Alps. Gerald's family refuses this request. This moment isn't retained in the film, instead ending with Ursula's painful realization that Birkin doesn't truly love her in the way that she wants, and never will.

While Lawrence engaged in same-sex relationships, he never approved of overt displays of homosexuality and repressed his own desires. This homoerotic relationship is more overt in the film, no doubt because of the changing views on homosexuality of the 1960s. A scene drawn from the novel wherein Birkin and Gerald engage in nude Japanese-style wrestling marked one of the first times full frontal male nudity was shown on-screen and colors the rest of the movie with its stark homoeroticism. The pair's nude grappling is both intimate and violent, culminating with a moment of peace between the two that's almost postcoital.

Critics at the time complained about the movie's overly simplified presentation of the book, a fact unsurprising considering how dense the six-hundred-page work is. Kramer and Russell were also disappointed in the finished product. Russell especially felt the movie wasn't his style and disagreed with Glenda Jackson's casting. However, *Women in Love* is such a complex novel that it's doubtful anyone could have translated it faithfully while keeping things interesting. As it stands, the film is a loving tribute to Lawrence as an author and provocateur.

Lawrence went on to write more novels, including *Lady Chatterley's Lover*, but none of them feel as bald-faced in their explorations of relationships and power dynamics as *Women in Love.*

LOVE STORY

1970

Directed by Arthur Hiller
Screenplay by Erich Segal
Based on *Love Story* by Erich Segal, 1970

"Love means never having to say you're sorry."

What can you say about a twenty-five-year-old girl who died?" The opening lines in Erich Segal's novel and script for *Love Story* immediately tell audiences where this story will end. The tale of wealthy WASP Oliver Barrett IV (Ryan O'Neal) and the Italian Catholic Jennifer Cavilleri (Ali MacGraw) is one that ends in her beautifully tragic demise, and yet watching the journey with that knowledge in mind is still incredibly powerful.

What makes *Love Story* a romance that's endured for fifty-five years is watching how the two characters grow, learn from each other's flaws, and stay together regardless of how little time they have. As director Arthur Hiller himself said about the movie, "The message of *Love Story* really is what two people can give to each other for love alone." Segal was inspired to write *Love Story* after hearing about a former student of his from Harvard who lost his wife to cancer at the age of twenty-five. Segal, an associate professor at Yale, conjured up a similar story that hearkened back to romantic melodramas of the 1940s like *Casablanca* (1942). "It deals with today's personal commitment of one to one and the quest for a permanent relationship which begins much younger than it used to," Segal said at the time.

Love Story is the adaptation equivalent of a "chicken or egg" scenario. It's disputed whether the novel was planned after the movie was already greenlit or not. Segal himself said he wrote the novel and the screenplay simultaneously. Some have said Segal initially wrote *Love Story* as a script but was unable to sell it. According to Robert Evans, then-president of Paramount as well as MacGraw's then-husband (they divorced in 1973), he suggested that Segal adapt the screenplay to help promote the film. Regardless, the novel dropped on Valentine's Day 1970 and became an instant success, setting the stage for the film's equally large box office that December.

The movie was a hot property, but casting it wasn't easy. Before O'Neal got the part, Jeff Bridges, Michael Douglas, and Jon Voight all refused the role of Oliver. MacGraw, as Jenny, was a different story. It's alleged that MacGraw herself discovered Segal's script because they were friends from college. When her husband, Robert Evans, agreed to produce the story, thinking "it might be a good, small, profitable trend-bucker," the implication was that MacGraw was guaranteed the lead role.

Because of how closely together the book and movie were written, there's very little distinguishing them. Even the amount of time it takes to read the book mimics the film's run time. "I cut [the book] to read in two hours because I wanted it to be a one-sitting experience, like the movie," Segal said. The movie lays out Jenny and Oliver's love story alongside Oliver's strained relationship with his father, Oliver Barrett III (Ray Milland). Oliver narrates the movie in flashback. The reader hears his inner thoughts and no one else's, with any information he gets about Jenny coming exclusively from her. Similar to Charles

Webb's *The Graduate*, published in 1963, hearing Oliver tell the story can, at times, make him come off as fairly unlikable. He is self-absorbed and entitled, thinking, "Why was I putting up with this? Doesn't [Jenny] read the *Crimson*? Doesn't she know who I am?" Oliver desperately doesn't want to be the arrogant snob Jenny perceives him to be—she constantly calls him "Preppie"—yet the reader sees his conscience undo him.

This ability to see Oliver completely, his feelings and actions, also allows the reader to view his relationship with his father differently. Because we don't get any insight into the mind of O. B. III—the nickname Oliver uses for his father—all we see is what looks like Oliver's constant annoyance at his dad. When Oliver's father drives all the way from Ithaca, New York, to Cambridge, Massachusetts, to watch his son play hockey, the younger man thinks his father is doing it to prove a point. O. B. III says Oliver enjoys being rebellious and it's impossible not to see that, especially as Oliver himself points it out: "I have no idea why I was putting myself down. Maybe it was because *he* was taking the opposite view." Even Jenny, who tries to reunite father and son after they have a falling-out, observes Oliver making assumptions about why she wants to bring them back together. He routinely brings up Jenny's Italian heritage in the book, explaining that she can only see their strained father/son dynamic through the lens of Italian families who have more close-knit relationships.

Jenny's mystery illness and death in the film was cited as overly hokey and sentimental by critics upon the film's release, with *New York Times* critic Vincent Canby saying that "Jenny was suffering from some vaguely unpleasant Elizabeth Arden treatment." The novel definitively states that Jenny is dying of leukemia, though Oliver tries hard to avoid telling anyone about her illness. At one point he gets a high-profile court case that he turns down because he doesn't want to leave her, but refuses to tell his boss what's going on.

Segal crafts a bitter moment of irony in the book when Jenny, after collapsing at the piano, tells Oliver that she needs to get to the hospital. Oliver ominously says he knows it'll be the last time she leaves the apartment. When they get into the cab and tell the driver where they're headed, the cabbie presumes Jenny is in labor; he perceives a moment of support that will lead to new life, while actually the moment is the culmination of death. Because the viewer isn't privy to Oliver's thoughts in the film, this moment is more painful on-screen.

Despite being savaged by critics, *Love Story* was the sixth-highest-grossing film of all time in the United States and Canada as of its release. Its soundtrack saw similar success, with a vocal rendition of its theme song, performed by Andy Williams, becoming a radio staple. The name "Jennifer" was a top baby name for the decade. That's not to mention the line "love means never having to say you're sorry" becoming a part of pop culture history. Hiller himself went to bat for the line, saying, "All it says is that if you love somebody, you understand they're not perfect and they don't have to apologize for every little thing they do that isn't perfect. It's an affirmation of the human spirit."

Segal returned to the world of Oliver Barrett IV with the 1977 book *Oliver's Story*, another romance showing Oliver trying to find love after Jenny; it was also turned into a feature in 1978, with O'Neal and Milland reprising their roles.

TESS

1979

Directed by Roman Polanski
Screenplay by Gérard Brach,
Roman Polanski, and John Brownjohn
Based on *Tess of the d'Urbervilles* by Thomas Hardy, 1891

"Beauty has its price."

Thomas Hardy's *Tess of the d'Urbervilles* straddles the line between nineteenth- and twentieth-century literature with its combination of the rigid sensibilities of the Victorian era with the complexity and emphasis on innovation that marked the Modernist era. The 1891 novel follows the title character, a young woman of strength and courage, albeit poor, whose family discovers they descend from a once-noble family, the d'Urbervilles. Hoping to use their newfound lineage to make their fortune, Tess's parents send her to her rich relatives to beg for money. The slick Alec d'Urberville, Tess's cousin, takes an instant shine to her and offers her a job. But when Alec sexually assaults Tess one evening, it puts her on a collision course with a series of tragedies that make her feel as if she is destined for doom.

Hardy's novel is unique for the time period as he sympathizes deeply with the lower classes, particularly the women struggling to survive in the country. Tess may not have a high-born name, but she shows the traits of a woman of good breeding: beauty, integrity, and bravery. The reader immediately bonds with her as she's put through the wringer of everything from sexual assault to the loss of a child and poverty. Hardy uses the ingrained feelings toward social class to cement Tess's journey as predetermined and unavoidable. Tess is poor and this is what the poor endure. Her family believes their newfound ancestry is set to change their destinies, but it only becomes the means of destroying their lives.

Tess of the d'Urbervilles has been adapted more for television than movie theaters, with the first American production going before cameras in 1913. It was made again in 1924, directed by Marshall Neilan, starring Blanche Sweet as Tess, Stuart Holmes as the villainous Alec, and Conrad Nagel as the kind, if overly judgmental, Angel Clare, Tess's beloved and eventual husband. Sadly, both this and the 1913 version are lost. It wasn't till the 1970s that another English-language version of the film was produced in Roman Polanski's *Tess*. Polanski wanted to adapt Hardy's novel in honor of his late wife, actress Sharon Tate, who loved the book and one day hoped to play Tess before her tragic murder in 1969. Polanski dedicates the film during its opening credits "To Sharon." He cast seventeen-year-old Nastassja Kinski (credited as Nastassia Kinski) in the title role, alongside Peter Firth as Angel and Leigh Lawson as Alec.

Polanski and longtime screenwriting partner Gérard Brach, alongside John Brownjohn, adapted Hardy's novel as faithfully as they could, with *Tess* clocking in at nearly three hours. Hardy goes into rich detail about the landscapes Tess and her family encounter so as to let the reader enter the story in as concrete a way as possible. Polanski was determined to make the settings evoke Hardy's blending of the modern and the Gothic. "To tell the story and all, it was essential to find the proper setting, a 20th-century equivalent of Hardy's 19th-century Dorset," said Polanski in an interview. The French locales of Brittany and Normandy were two of the eighty locations used to mimic Hardy's Dorset, England.

Polanski and Hardy focus on the destruction of innocence and how oppression affects people. A key element in the book is Tess's sexual assault by Alec, a scene Hardy treats without judgment, anathema for his time considering that any sexual situations a woman was engaged in, regardless of consent, left her reputation tainted. Tess is violated in the book while asleep and the narrator considers her "disgrace" a fated element that is part of the world she inhabits. If the universe is conspiring against her, then she is not responsible for what's happened and shouldn't be judged for it. The film version of this scene is similarly respectful, though Tess is awake when the assault takes place. She kisses Alec only to realize she doesn't want to go any further. The camera focuses on her hands curling into fists as mist envelops the pair.

Hardy's novel was serialized, a common technique for writers of his period. Each of the book's seven "phases" tells a specific story within the larger narrative of Tess's life. The book alternates sections that build to a climax, with the following section showing the consequences of said climax. Since Tess presumes so much of her life is being destroyed by fate, Hardy brings in all manner of coincidences for her to encounter to make it seem as if fate is conspiring against her. Examples include Tess's father and mother getting drunk in celebration of their newfound ancestry and forcing Tess to take the family horse to do a job. The horse ends up dying in an accident and Tess, out of guilt, decides to visit the d'Urbervilles to help her family, setting the plot in motion.

Tess's script eliminates several of these coincidences, particularly Angel's parents, who believe Tess too lowly to marry their son. In the movie Alec is a newfound preacher when Tess meets him, while in the book Angel's father is a preacher who tells Angel he's having trouble converting a particularly rascally soul by the name of Alec d'Uberville. Alec's character is limited to necessary scenes in the movie, like the assault and his coercion of Tess into being his mistress before she murders him. When Tess starts working at a dairy farm, people talk about a charismatic preacher who happens to be Alec. His conversion to Christianity and job as a preacher—which Tess condemns him for, believing it to be an attempt to secure his place in heaven—are removed.

Also removed are Hardy's Gothic elements that can make things overly macabre in a book that already has so much tragedy and violence in it. After Tess confesses about her rape, and how she bore a son named Sorrow who died the morning after Tess named and christened him, Angel rejects her. He then sleepwalks in the night, picks Tess up, and carries her to a nearby churchyard, where he places her in an empty coffin. Hardy isn't subtle with his metaphors and this moment literally manifests that Tess is dead to Angel, while also foreshadowing her own execution for Alec's murder. Alec has violated Tess physically, but Angel sees Tess's past as violating his spirituality.

Tess of the d'Urbervilles is about battling fate, particularly as a woman also grappling with societal expectations. Tess strives to be good and also seeks a companion who won't judge her for the cruel hand fate has dealt her. She believes she's found it with Angel. Angel realizes the error of his ways and redeems Tess, but she is still persecuted. Tess becomes too saintly for the world and the love she is set to receive in Heaven is far more secure and true than anything on Earth.

Hardy was well regarded for *Tess of the d'Urbervilles* as well as his follow-up novel *Jude the Obscure*, but he always saw himself more as a poet, writing novels to pay the bills. The controversy that came from his two most famous works and their pessimistic views of Victorian society compelled him to give up book writing and stay in the world of poetry for the rest of his life. For Polanski, the film's nine-month shoot on location made it the most expensive French production at that time, with a budget of $12 million. *Tess* was nominated for ten Academy Awards, winning three, for Best Cinematography (Geoffrey Unsworth and Ghislain Cloquet), Best Art Direction/ Set Decoration (Pierre Guffroy and Jack Stephens), and Best Costume Design (Anthony Powell).

SOMEWHERE IN TIME

1980

Directed by Jeannot Szwarc
Screenplay by Richard Matheson
Based on *Bid Time Return* by Richard Matheson, 1975

"Please, don't leave. You have no idea how far I've come to be with you."

Like its narrative, *Somewhere in Time* inhabits two worlds: both a romantic drama and a sci-fi story, penned by prolific horror and sci-fi writer Richard Matheson. Best known for writing *I Am Legend*, *The Incredible Shrinking Man*, and *Hell House* (as well as being the screenwriter behind some of the best episodes of *The Twilight Zone*), Matheson was inspired to write *Somewhere in Time* after visiting Piper's Opera House in Nevada where he stumbled upon a photo of Maude Adams, an actress popular in the 1890s–1900s, and creatively fell in love with her, inspiring him to write a novel based around the experience. He brought that same beauty between love and science to the script, adapting his own novel for the screen.

The story follows Richard Collier (Christopher Reeve), a writer in 1980 who learns he's dying from brain cancer. He travels to the storied Grand Hotel, where he falls deeply in love with a photograph of a stage actress named Elise McKenna (Jane Seymour), who lived in 1912. His desire to be with her compels him to mentally will himself back into the past. Once there, he meets Elise and her possessive manager William Robinson (Christopher Plummer). But can Richard, a man of the twentieth century, maintain his grip on the past and the love he has with Elise?

The book and film focus on love's ability to transcend time and space, as well the role destiny plays in relationships. Long, eloquently written passages detail Richard's questions and fears about traveling back in time. Will his arrival affect future events? Even the nature of their relationship is a paradox. In the present, Richard learns that Gustav Mahler is Elise's favorite composer, but Richard turns out to be the one who actually introduces Elise to Mahler's music. Their relationship is one that is not necessarily preordained, but it is inevitable. Like any good soulmate, each is destined to find the other no matter what. Elise tells Richard of two separate interactions she's had with psychics who predicted a man would come and change her life. (Matheson focused on this again, albeit involving the afterlife, in his 1978 novel *What Dreams May Come*.)

Matheson sets the novel at the Hotel del Coronado near San Diego, the hotel famously seen in Billy Wilder's *Some Like It Hot* (1959). For Richard, it's the place where he wants to spend his last days before he dies (the tumor is entirely absent in the movie). But due to the modernity in and surrounding the Hotel del Coronado by the time filming began, the movie couldn't utilize the location and so turned to the Grand Hotel on the isolated Mackinac Island in Michigan, which is where the movie is set. The film also pushes the events of the book forward, having Richard travel back to 1912 instead of 1896, and setting it in the summer as opposed to the colder month of November.

Richard reads in a biography on Elise that she "stands for all that represents true and virtuous womanhood." Seymour's performance in the film certainly represents that, with her astounding beauty and charm making her the ideal woman. In the book, Elise is forced to hide who she is and what she values due to the time period. She reveals to Richard that she believes in women's suffrage and is shocked to hear he does too.

Elise has more personality and individuality on the page, but the film makes her an active participant in the narrative with Richard. The movie includes her in sequences that she is absent from in the book. Richard accidentally discovers a penny from 1971 in his coat pocket, a reminder that he doesn't belong there. It breaks his connection to the past and sends him back to the present. The movie has Elise witness it first-hand, in the room with Richard when he disappears, whereas the book has her asleep. The movie opens with an old woman confronting Richard while he's in college, a moment he doesn't understand but that will soon make sense to the viewer: By being in the room and witnessing Richard disappear, the viewer realizes Elise is on her own quest to reunite with him.

In the book, when Richard returns to the present he's only been gone ten to fifteen minutes, not several days as depicted in the film. Richard leaves the hotel dejected to have lost his one true love. The book, composed of Richard's journal entries, ends up posthumously released by his brother, Robert, who doesn't believe the story is true but says Richard believed it was. Like any good Matheson story, the novel ends on an ambiguous note: Did Richard go back in time? Or was this the dreamlike fantasy of a dying man? Matheson's script for the movie goes for pure romanticism, with Richard returning to the present, his body emaciated and dying from lack of food and drink for what appears to be weeks of neglect. He dies in the hotel to be reunited with Elise in the afterlife. Matheson's film script ends not unlike a ghost story in which the lovers are together forever, haunting the location where they first fell in love.

Actress Jane Seymour said during a screening of the movie at the 2022 TCM Classic Film Festival that it wasn't hard to feign chemistry with her costar Christopher Reeve, as the two ended up falling "madly in love" while making the feature.

Somewhere in Time was not a success when it hit theaters in 1980. Seymour and Reeve were prohibited from promoting the movie due to a SAG-AFTRA strike and the film's distributor, Universal Pictures, was more financially invested in *The Blues Brothers* (1980), leaving *Somewhere in Time* with a small marketing budget. It wasn't until the movie was sold to television that audiences discovered the beauty and magic of the film, as well as Matheson's writing. The author wrote eighteen more books after *Somewhere in Time* before his passing in 2013. With many of his works becoming films, he is one of the most adapted authors of his generation.

THE FRENCH LIEUTENANT'S WOMAN

1981

Directed by Karel Reisz
Screenplay by Harold Pinter
Based on *The French Lieutenant's Woman*
by John Fowles, 1969

"Now that I know there was truly a day upon which you loved me, I can bear anything."

A sweeping English landscape, a woman getting ready in a makeup chair, and a clapperboard signaling the beginning of a film shoot. Within the confines of this film production the audience follows the story of a couple living in nineteenth-century England, unable to be together due to the social mores of the time. The actors playing them, carrying on an illicit affair of their own, are similarly bound by societal strictures despite times being more sexually open. These are the two stories at play within director Karel Reisz's adaptation of *The French Lieutenant's Woman*. Jeremy Irons portrays the actor Mike, as well as the buttoned-up Charles Smithson in the movie they're making, while Meryl Streep is Anna off-screen and has the role of the fallen woman, Sarah Woodruff.

John Fowles's 1969 novel was originally considered unfilmable due to its postmodernist style, which includes extensive footnotes about various topics, from Victorian-era history to philosophy and Darwinism, plus an omniscient narrator who is constantly interrupting the story in the hopes of controlling the characters. It's easy to understand that, despite Fowles's popularity with the release of his 1963 book *The Collector*—itself adapted into a stellar film in 1965 directed by William Wyler—*French Lieutenant* was considered difficult. Midway through the book, the narrator—implied to be Fowles himself—reveals, "This story I am telling is all in my imagination. These characters I create never existed outside my own mind." For the narrator, the point of writing the book is to "stand next to God" while "[creating] worlds as real as, but other than the world that is." So the story of *The French Lieutenant's Woman*, on the page, is one that attempts to emulate the Victorian-era novel and the landscape of the time while being cognizant of the period in which the author is writing it—this being the 1960s. Fowles uses actual novels and poems as source material to assert the reality of the times, and writes the characters as if they truly existed.

The book doesn't have the film-within-a-film structure, and the narrator works to erase his own mistakes or comment on situations where the reader might ask questions. Sarah contemplates suicide at one point, only for the narrator to say, "We know she didn't because she was seen later." Who determines this? Is Sarah a person who exists and has history? Or is this just another moment when the narrator is thinking out loud about the character and doesn't want to box himself into a corner? The book is also peppered with several humorous asides where the narrator pokes fun at the characters and the times they live in. "[I]t is no wonder that duty has become such a key concept in our understanding of the Victorian age—or for that matter, such a wet blanket in our own," he says at one point.

Fowles wanted director Karel Reisz to direct the movie, initially approaching him in 1969. Reisz had already received critical acclaim for his features *Saturday Night and Sunday Morning* (1960) and *Isadora* (1968). When he finally decided to tackle the project, he was stumped by how to translate the novel's awareness that it was a book into the film space. Enter playwright and screenwriter Harold Pinter. Pinter was well versed in blending subtext into a story and working with unique narrative structures, as evidenced by his writing for features like *The Servant* (1963) and *The Pumpkin Eater* (1964). Reisz conjured up the idea of telling the story of Charles and Sarah through two actors playing their parts, and from there Pinter gave audiences what they see on-screen.

Adding Mike and Anna as modern-day counterparts to the Victorian characters they're playing shows how social mores have changed (or are solidified) in modern romance. These themes are seen in the novel, where Fowles plays them up to more exaggerated proportions. Charles is high-class, descending from a baronet. Sarah, called "the French Lieutenant's whore" by the townspeople of Lyme, is forced to wear the shame of her presumed promiscuity. That, coupled with her low social standing, leaves Charles torn between his own personal feelings for her and his desire to adhere to the status quo. When his uncle is set to marry, Charles and his fiancée Ernestina (Lynsey Baxter) worry about what this means for Charles's social position. Charles thinks of Ernestina strictly in terms of her money and his ability to sleep with her, but with Sarah he appreciates how she reminds him of what he lacks in life: love and happiness. He also is compelled to save her, putting him in the position of savior.

As the tragic beauty, Sarah has a masochistic love of being shamed, if only because it allows her to forget that she is an educated woman whose only profession is marriage. "You are not a woman who was born to be a farmer's wife but educated to be something . . . better," Sarah tells Charles. She comes off more like a feminist of the 1960s than a woman of the Victorian era. The novel is less about love between its characters and more about how things like marriage and class cause couples to sublimate parts of themselves, no matter the time period. Mike feels that even though he and Anna are married to other people, he is willing to forsake what people think for love. Anna, on the other hand, doesn't want to be labeled "a whore" like the woman she's portraying.

Fowles's narrator says his characters gain autonomy as the story unfolds and he can't disrespect their choices if he wants them to be real. As such, Fowles gives the reader multiple endings and multiple choices for how Sarah and Charles's lives turn out. The first ending sees Charles and Sarah part forever after they spend the night together. Charles confesses everything about his relationship with Sarah to Ernestina, and they end up marrying and having two sons. All's well that ends well.

In the next two endings, Fowles literally inserts himself as a new character into the story, watching everything play out. Sarah leaves town and, after Charles spends twenty months searching for her, the two are reunited. In one ending, Sarah rejects marrying Charles but tells him that she bore his child, a daughter named Lalage. Charles meets Lalage and, though it's ambiguous, the implication is that he and Sarah end up together. The third and final ending sees Sarah reject Charles's entreaties of marriage, whereupon Charles, in anger, leaves the house never knowing about Lalage's existence. Whichever ending the reader prefers is up to them. The film condenses this down to only two endings: one in which Sarah and Charles end up together and, after the fictional movie wraps up, Mike discovers Anna has left him forever. Mike cries "Sarah" as Anna's car drives away, the lines between film and reality blurred beyond repair.

John Fowles once wrote about the function of *The French Lieutenant's Woman*, "You are not trying to write something one of the Victorian novelists forgot to write; but perhaps something one of them failed to write." Fowles and director Karel Reisz (with Pinter's script) do this very thing. Both versions of *The French Lieutenant's Woman* are not representative of the Victorian era, but show a new way of looking at relationships of their respective times. It's also a fantastic exploration of how the style of romantic literature takes established genre conventions and plays with them. Each version is romantic and entertaining in its own way.

OUT OF AFRICA

1985

Directed by Sydney Pollack
Screenplay by Kurt Luedtke
Based on *Out of Africa* by Karen Blixen, 1937

"Perhaps he knew, as I did not, that the Earth was made round so that we would not see too far down the road."

Denys loved to hear a story told well," Karen Blixen (Meryl Streep) says at the beginning of 1985's *Out of Africa*. The story that unfolds is certainly told well, filled with all manner of lust, excitement, tragedy, and beauty set against the background of a lush African landscape. Director Sydney Pollack's adaptation of Blixen's 1937 memoir is a sweeping tale of romance and adventure that follows Blixen's move from her native Denmark to Africa. Once there, she attempts to turn her farm into a thriving coffee plantation while beginning a love affair with big-game hunter Denys Finch-Hatton (Robert Redford).

Blixen's original book, penned under her pseudonym Isak Dinesen, is less a narrative memoir than it is a series of anecdotes about her life. As Karen tells Denys in the movie, she fancies herself akin to Scheherazade, the storyteller in *One Thousand and One Nights* known for weaving beautiful and intricate stories. Karen shares her stories in small, self-contained chunks, each with a beginning, a middle, and an end that, on their own, point to specific themes in her life, and, taken altogether, present a multilayered tale.

The book is broken up into five distinct parts, focusing on specific elements of the African landscape, its people, and history. Karen spends several chapters looking at the legal system held by the native villagers and how it compares to the European justice system. The stories soon become brief observations and stray accounts, none interconnected or seeming to have any bearing on the plot, short of touching on Blixen's interest in Africa as an idyllic pastoral landscape and her loving interactions with the natives that work her property. The character who changes Karen's life and with whom she falls in love—Denys—doesn't even arrive till the fourth section of the book, when the narrative finally turns chronological and reaches its bittersweet and tragic conclusion.

Blixen writes like an anthropologist, so much had to be changed to bring the movie to the screen. Upon the US publication of *Out of Africa* in 1938, Hollywood was eager to translate it and planned it as a vehicle for Greta Garbo. At various points in time Orson Welles, David Lean, and Nicolas Roeg planned to direct. Roeg appears to have gotten the furthest along, with Julie Christie and Ryan O'Neal in mind as Blixen and Finch-Hatton.

When Pollack approached the property, he understood Blixen's novel needed some serious beefing up considering how anecdotal it is. Rather than limit himself to *Out of Africa* as the only source material, Pollack wove in elements from Judith Thurman's biography on Blixen, *Isak Dinesen: The Life of a Storyteller*, and Errol Trzebinski's biography on Finch-Hatton, *Silence Will Speak*; all three are credited on the finished film. Only about six events from Blixen's work are translated directly into the movie, with the first two sections of narration performed by Streep being direct quotes from Blixen's book. Subsequent narrations were penned by Oscar-winning screenwriter Kurt Luedtke to mimic Blixen's lyrical writing style.

Blixen doesn't tell the reader much of anything about herself. The book never indicates when it takes place or why she's there. She never introduces herself or gives us any name to call her short of "the narrator." Even her gender isn't clear until one of her young servants, Kamante (Joseph Thiaka) calls her "Msabu," a native term for a white woman. The reader doesn't even know the narrator is married until she reveals that she's delivering supplies to her husband during World War I, a scene also shown in the movie.

Blixen's relationship with Denys requires a close reading in the book, as the author never specifically indicates any romantic relationship between the two. While Karen had already divorced her husband, Baron Bror Blixen (Klaus Maria Brandauer) in 1925, etiquette prohibited her from flagrantly showing off her relationship with Denys. Part of Karen's progression on-screen is her refusal to be an old maid by marrying Bror, a man with whom she is friendly, but not in love. She later must decide whether she's willing to accept an independent life with Denys that doesn't include marriage.

Karen and Denys's relationship in the film is old-fashioned but highly romantic, in the vein of Redford's previous films like *The Way We Were*. Redford's casting is jarring if one does research on the real Denys Finch-Hatton, who is described as an English aristocrat, the son of the 13th Earl of Winchilsea. Blixen praises his regal bearing and considers him to have the bluest of blood. The American-born Redford was picked more for his charm and his established relationship with Pollack than anything else. Redford, to his credit, attempted a British accent early in the filming process, but Pollack thought it was distracting and told him to stop doing it, requiring some of his early scenes to be redubbed.

The film eschews much of the reality of the pair's relationship, like the fact that Karen had at least two pregnancies and miscarriages during her relationship with Denys, or that he was away from Africa for two full years doing military service in Egypt. And unlike the movie, in which Denys dies in a plane crash days before Karen leaves Africa, the events actually occurred three months apart.

Because of the time period in which the book was written, Blixen projects all her passion onto the environment to subtly detail to the reader what her relationship with Denys is like. She alludes to her pure lust for him in a passage that describes his return to the Dinesen farm. She talks about how the farm responds the same way African plants do "when with the first showers of the rainy season they flower, dripping wet, a cloud of chalk." This same sexual metaphor also manifests when the pair are hunting, where she blends sex and sport. Karen sees a lioness eating a dead giraffe and tells Denys to shoot it, which he does. When the pair drives back through the area later, they see a lion eating the same carcass. Once again, Karen tells Denys to kill the lion and he does. As the servants skin the lions, the pair has lunch. The narrator's lust for hunting is a sign of feminine sexuality, while Denys's experience as a hunter speaks to his male virility. In the movie, Denys specifically doesn't shoot any animal he doesn't have to and refuses to shoot a lioness coming toward Karen because he knows that, if given time, it will move on. It isn't until the pair are directly confronted by a pair of lions that he is forced to shoot. The alteration appears to be the result of 1980s mores against big-game hunting and support for animal conservation, not to mention wanting to avoid making the charismatic and romantic Redford look callous.

Blixen's book isn't about a love for a person so much as it is a love for a location. Though dated in its white colonialist worldview, it attempts to show the beauty of Africa. The movie still is hampered by a white savior narrative, but pivots by creating a love story between two adventure seekers who find love amid the beauty of a foreign land.

Out of Africa was a serious awards darling in 1985, nominated for eleven Academy Awards and winning seven, including Best Picture, Director (Pollack), Adapted Screenplay, Cinematography, Art Direction, Sound, and Score. It ushered in a slew of similar period romances, most famously the 1996 film *The English Patient* and 1995's *The Bridges of Madison County*, also starring Streep.

A ROOM WITH A VIEW

1985

Directed by James Ivory
Screenplay by Ruth Prawer Jhabvala
Based on *A Room with a View* by E. M. Forster, 1908

"You love George. You love the boy, body and soul, as he loves you."

A young girl walks into a poppy field in Italy. Looking down, she sees a young man lost in reflection. Struck by the immense beauty that surrounds him, he turns and spots the girl. He strides up to her and plants a kiss. The kiss among the poppies between Lucy Honeychurch (Helena Bonham Carter) and George Emerson (Julian Sands) is an unforgettably romantic scene in the Merchant Ivory–produced adaptation of E. M. Forster's novel *A Room with a View.*

The novel, a bildungsroman, and film follow the young and naive Lucy as she tours Italy with her cousin/companion Charlotte Bartlett (Maggie Smith). The two arrive at their Italian hotel only to discover that the "room with a view" they've been promised isn't what they've received. Thus kicks off a series of interactions with the melancholy George and his father, Mr. Emerson (Denholm Elliott), who offer Lucy and Charlotte their own room with said view. Lucy and George have an attraction to each other, but issues of social standing and temperament get in the way. Lucy returns to London, where she is set to marry the snobbish Cecil Vyse (Daniel Day-Lewis), but when George and his father end up in the same location Lucy is torn over which man she truly loves.

Having lost his father at the age of two, Edward Morgan Forster was raised by his strong-willed mother and great-aunt, each woman an inspiration for the headstrong leading ladies of Forster's books, of which Lucy Honeychurch is one. Forster wrote *A Room with a View* between the years 1901 and 1902 at the age of twenty-two, inspired by his own trip to Italy. But the novel wouldn't be published until 1908.

Similar to the works of Henry James, Forster's novel is a romance as well as a comic look into the transition away from the stodgy thinking of Queen Victoria's time and toward the more liberal social behavior of the contemporary era. The various hotel guests Lucy meets in Italy are described as the "better class of tourist" compared to those visiting the country and staying in lesser accommodations. They all come from wealthy and better-educated families of good social standing, with the exception of the Emersons, who are perceived as more common in both their social status and their inability to adhere to the right type of social conventions. Because the novel is told through a third-person omniscient narrator, the reader is exposed to what the rich characters are thinking, revealing their petty snobberies toward lower-class British citizens and the Italians. Forster uses this device to slyly poke fun at or undermine them. The only ones whose thoughts the reader isn't privy to are George and his father.

Screenwriter Ruth Prawer Jhabvala doesn't change much from Forster's book, but the loss of the omniscient narrator means that much of the author's humor doesn't come through,

and the snobbishness of the wealthy characters is either absent or manifested through dialogue. Much of Forster's incisive exploration of class is also absent.

Lucy's decision between the prim and boring Cecil and the free-spirited George is where the film's biggest class conflicts lie. The kiss in the poppy field? It might shock you to know that doesn't happen in the book, which sees Lucy go out to a terrace covered in blue violets, where she finds George standing on the terrace's edge "like a swimmer while he prepares." There, the kiss happens. Forster describes the terrace as "the primal source whence beauty gushed out to water the Earth," with the kiss from George representing all that is uncivilized, raw, and beautiful that can occur when social barriers are transcended.

It's a beautifully written passage, but jarring considering the poppy field is such an evocative image in the movie.

At its core, Lucy and George's romance is about transcending social conventions. George starts the book as melancholy before Italy revitalizes him. He never does the right thing, according to Lucy, and acts impulsively. Yet Lucy is attracted to this, especially in comparison with the buttoned-up Cecil.

Jhabvala is able to give more time to characters who don't have much to do in Forster's novel, such as Lucy's cousin Charlotte. Charlotte is a shy old maid in the book, who is revealed to have forsaken her own grand love; it is initially presumed she will to encourage Lucy to do the same. Charlotte is the linchpin to the book's ending, with George and Lucy questioning whether she intentionally made certain decisions in the hopes of bringing them together. The book leaves it ambiguous as to whether Charlotte was there to push Lucy into love or not. On-screen, things are even more ambiguous.

As played by Maggie Smith in the film, Charlotte has a more nuanced personality—she is proper but also wistful—and is given several additional scenes that originally just had Lucy in them. One example is when gossipy writer Eleanor Lavish (Judi Dench) takes a walk through a small town in Florence. In the novel, Eleanor and Lucy take this walk together. Eleanor refuses to let Lucy use her Baedaker tour book to guide their way and they promptly get lost. The film changes the scene to Eleanor and Charlotte. This gives Charlotte more to do, but it also gives her a companion in Eleanor. The romantic author contrasts and complements the buttoned-up Charlotte, giving the latter an outlet for a romantic fantasy life Charlotte wishes she could experience.

George also gets a few additional moments of character in the novel, such as a passage detailing his first memory of his late mother and father looking out into the distance, hearkening back to how the various characters all seek "a view" they wish to look at in life.

Hollywood desperately wanted to adapt Forster's novels, particularly *A Room with a View*, going back to 1946 when Twentieth Century Fox offered $25,000 to Forster himself for the rights. The author didn't think cinema was a highbrow medium and refused. Upon Forster's death in 1970 the rights to his books transferred to the board of fellows at King's College, Cambridge, who refused to entertain any film offers. When a new chief executor was brought on in 1980, the rights were finally sold to director James Ivory and his producing partner, Ismail Merchant. Merchant described *A Room with a View* as "the film that catapulted us [Merchant Ivory] from the art house to the multiplex." The debut of *A Room with a View* in 1985, on the heels of the prior year's well-regarded adaptation of Forster's *A Passage to India* from David Lean, sparked a surge of Forster adaptations. Two years later, Merchant Ivory released a film version of Forster's *Maurice* (1987).

A Room with a View was nominated for eight Oscars, winning three: for Jhabvala's script, the costumes, and art/set decoration. Ivory, Merchant, and Jhabvala worked together on seven more features after *A Room with a View*, including an adaptation of another Forster novel, *Howards End* (1992), and *The Remains of the Day* (1993), an adaptation of the Kazuo Ishiguro novel. Their last project as a trio was the 2003 feature *Le Divorce*. In 2005, Ismail Merchant died at the age of sixty-eight, and Ruth Prawar Jhabvala passed away in 2013 at the age of eighty-five. James Ivory continues to work on films, most recently writing the script for the 2017 adaptation of André Aciman's queer romance *Call Me by Your Name*, directed by Luca Guadagnino.

The romance of Lucy Honeychurch and George Emerson never looks as lusciously beautiful as it did when Merchant Ivory brought it to the screen. Forster set the tone, and they brought it to stunning life.

MAURICE

1987
Directed by James Ivory
Screenplay by Kit Hesketh-Harvey and James Ivory
Based on *Maurice* by E. M. Forster, 1971

"Now, we shan't never be parted. It's finished."

E. M. Forster's final book, *Maurice*, was a groundbreaking LGBTQ+ novel upon its publication after the author's death in 1971. But it would take sixteen years after for it to be adapted into a motion picture.

The story follows Cambridge student Maurice Hall (James Wilby), who falls in love with fellow schoolmate Clive Durham (Hugh Grant). As the pair's relationship develops over the years, Maurice's conflicting views on his sexuality force him to deal with his identity and discover what love truly looks like.

Like *A Room with a View*, *Maurice* is also a bildungsroman, the reader seeing the transformation of the central character from youth to adulthood. We first meet young Maurice when he's fourteen (eleven in the film), just as he gets his first inkling of what sex is and the growing changes he'll experience once puberty hits. Maurice is confused about his attraction to boys when he discovers that George, a servant boy who used to play with him, has been sent away. He feels a deep sense of loss but doesn't understand what the heartbreak means. Because the book charts Maurice's development, we spend significant time with him as a teenager, unlike in the movie, which moves directly from Maurice as a child to his time as a college student. The book and film walk a similar path after this, with Maurice meeting Clive, whom the book describes as "a small man" with "simple manners and a fair face."

Forster initially wrote the novel between 1913 and 1914, with edits in 1932 and 1959–1960, so the interactions between Clive and Maurice on the page are chaste and given narrative weight due to Clive's belief that same-sex relationships should be strictly platonic. Yet the reader gets snatches of their closeness that aren't seen in the movie, such as Clive and Maurice traveling together arm in arm. Clive has been aware that he's gay since he was a boy, the book says, but feels it's a punishment from God. He has spent much of his childhood believing himself to be damned and, at sixteen, has a nervous breakdown. He believes he has corrupted Maurice through their relationship and, after falling ill briefly, commits himself to heterosexuality. "I have become normal," he tells Maurice.

None of Clive's history is in the movie, so it's up to Hugh Grant's performance to convey Clive's inner torment at denying his love for Maurice. Clive and Maurice's romantic relationship comes to an end in the movie after their friend Risley (Mark Tandy) is arrested and sent to jail for soliciting sex from a soldier. Clive fears he'll be exposed by his friendship with Risley, so he breaks up with Maurice and quickly marries the shy Anne (Phoebe Nicholls). Clive marries Anne in Forster's book, but Risley is a minor figure who is never caught or imprisoned for anything. It was Ivory's longtime writing partner, Ruth Prawer Jhabvala, who suggested utilizing Risley as a catalyst for the couple's breakup since there is none in the novel.

Maurice pursues women throughout the book, specifically Gladys Olcott, a young lady who visits his family's house. But his attempts to show her affection are too aggressive and Gladys states that "his touch revolted her. It was a corpse's." Rejected by Gladys, Maurice resolves to become completely celibate and eschew the company of men entirely. "He had been forewarned and therefore forearmed," the narrator writes. "And had only to keep away from boys and young men to ensure success."

However, Maurice starts seeing Dickie, the nephew of his family doctor, Dr. Barry (Denholm Elliott). "He mistook Dickie for a second Clive," the narrator says, making it obvious why Maurice is quick to fall in love with him. But Maurice realizes Dickie is not like Clive and his ardor for him cools. Scenes with Dickie's character were filmed but cut from the movie.

Maurice believes he'll never find anyone as good as Clive, let alone someone who understands him. But that changes when he gets into a relationship with the under-gamekeeper of Clive's estate, a working-class man named Alec Scudder (Rupert Graves). The pair have an instant attraction, but when Alec says he's planning to emigrate to Argentina, Maurice is prepared to forsake his reputation and social position for him.

Forster refused to end the book unhappily, unlike other works that persecuted their homosexual characters, so Maurice discovers Alec didn't get on the boat for Argentina and the pair commit themselves to each other. When Maurice reveals to Clive in the book that he and Alec are together, Clive tries to dissuade Maurice from living openly as a gay man. Clive even contemplates paying Alec off trying to convince Maurice to marry. Maurice and Alec get their happy ending, but the reader is left to see Clive is doomed to a life of unhappiness, denying himself and trying to convince the man he once loved to live a lie with him. The movie ends similarly but with more subtlety as Clive accepts that he and Maurice will never be together. He is left to return to his chaste, cold relationship with his wife.

Forster was open about his homosexuality with his closest friends, but he never sought to publish *Maurice* during his lifetime, seeing it as unpublishable due to the public and legal attitudes toward homosexuality. It was published in 1970, just three years after homosexuality was decriminalized in the United Kingdom.

When the filmmaking team of producer Ismail Merchant and director/screenwriter James Ivory approached King's College, Cambridge—the rights holders for all of E. M. Forster's work—about adapting *Maurice*, the college was hesitant. Not due to the novel's subject matter, but because Forster and his critics considered it an inferior work. No such claims were made against the movie. Critics celebrated the film for being accepting of homosexuality and depicting the characters' sexuality frankly and honestly, particularly when the gay community was being demonized due to the AIDS epidemic.

Forster's novel is a remarkably progressive exploration of same-sex relationships in the 1900s presented with tenderness and authenticity. Maurice's search to live his life as he chooses, and find a lover who accepts him, remains a universal story.

LIKE WATER FOR CHOCOLATE

1992

Directed by Alfonso Arau
Screenplay by Laura Esquivel
Based on *Like Water for Chocolate* by Laura Esquivel, 1989

"Tita, my great aunt. She will continue to live as long as someone cooks her recipes."

The magic of first love is a unique feeling. What could be a metaphorical use of magic to describe it manifests literally through the food of Tita (Lumi Cavazos), the heroine of author Laura Esquivel's 1989 novel *Like Water for Chocolate*. Tita is the youngest of three daughters, and because she is the last child, her mother, Elena (Regina Torné), declares Tita will never marry or have children. Her only job is to care for Elena till she dies. Unfortunately, Tita is in love with Pedro (Marco Leonardi), who loves her in return and wishes to marry her. Mama Elena offers Pedro an alternative: to marry Tita's older sister Rosaura (Yareli Arizmendi). Their marriage forces Tita to go on a journey toward finding her own identity and, along the way, her emotions start to wildly come through in the food she creates for her family.

Esquivel's *Like Water for Chocolate* is an example of the literary genre of magical realism established by Cuban writer Alejo Carpentier in 1949. Magical realism fiction sees supernatural and/or fantastical elements coexist in the real world. As writer Luis Leal describes it, "Its aim, unlike that of magic, is to express emotions, not to evoke them." Magic is used to make a point, concurrently explore Latin America's history with European colonialism, and help the characters communicate their emotions.

As the book and movie show, whenever Tita represses her feelings they come through in her cooking. Tita, told not to cry on the day of Pedro and Rosaura's wedding, loses a few tears in the batter of their wedding cake. These tears cause everyone who eats the cake to weep over their own lost loves before vomiting. When Pedro gives Tita flowers (in front of her mother in the movie and privately in the book), Tita uses them to make a rose petal sauce for the family dinner. Upon eating it, Pedro's lust for Tita comes through the rose petals and is infused into the meal, so much so that Tita's older sister Gertrudis (Claudette Maillé) becomes overcome by it. In the movie, an extreme steam heat exudes from her during a shower in their outhouse. A Mexican revolutionary smells her "rose scent" while riding by on a horse. The sheer amount of heat causes the outhouse to catch fire, forcing Gertrudis to flee in the nude, whereupon the revolutionary, finding her on his ride, scoops her up onto his horse and runs away with

her. The book goes even further, having Gertrudis exude pink sweat, with the water from the shower evaporating off her body because she is so hot.

Esquivel adapted her own novel for the movie and, at the time, was director Alfonso Arau's wife. Nearly the entirety of the book makes its way onto the screen, with the exception of Mama Elena's fate. Elena is callously thrown off a cliff by bandits in the movie while trying to save the family's maid, Chencha (Pilar Aranda), from being raped. Tita, who has run away from the family ranch after refusing to be physically and emotionally abused by her mother any longer, returns home for the funeral. The book sees Elena become a paraplegic after the attack and Tita returns to nurse her back to health. Elena is disgusted and humiliated by Tita's return and refuses to eat anything her daughter cooks, believing it's poisoned. After a month, Elena dies from what is discovered to be self-induced consumption of ipecac, poisoned and killed by the very thing she used to stave off poisoning.

Other select changes were made to soften the more overt symbolic passages that work best on the page, like the near out-of-body experience Tita has on Pedro and Rosaura's wedding day as she fixates on the white wedding dress and cake. The abundance of different spirits that pop up in Tita's life is also limited. The movie shows Tita visited by Elena's spirit after her death, with the audience left to interpret whether this is a real ghost or Tita's repressed thoughts rising to the surface. In the book, Tita encounters another spirit after a mental breakdown she endures as she recuperates in the house of a kindhearted doctor, John Brown (Mario Iván Martínez). The spirit, a silent woman, is revealed to be John's grandmother, an Indigenous woman named Morning Light, who inspired John's interest in science and medicine.

Compared to Elena's cruel spirit, Morning Light understands Tita's mental fragility and situates John's house as a place of comfort.

Tita is determined to be the last daughter affected by Elena's rule, though Rosaura wants to continue the tradition with her daughter Esperanza. The novel jumps ahead several years to Tita working on the wedding of Esperanza and Alex Brown, John Brown's son. In the movie, Rosaura dies of an unknown stomach ailment while Esperanza is an infant. The book's narrator implies that Rosaura sees her daughter grow into adulthood, at which time Tita and Pedro beg her to let Esperanza marry. After days of arguing with the two, Rosaura dies. In another bit of comic irony, the book's narrator says Rosaura's funeral was poorly attended because her body exuded an unbearable smell, Rosaura's bitterness and unhappiness still giving off a scent after death.

Though the book's narrator is never disclosed, the movie reveals that Esperanza's daughter is the one telling the story to the viewer. For Tita and Pedro, though they are finally able to be together after Rosaura's death, the movie shows their love as short-lived, with Pedro dying of a heart attack while consummating their relationship. Tita refuses to live without him and eats several matches, spontaneously combusting.

Esperanza's daughter relies on oral tradition, the process of telling stories, as a means of keeping Pedro and Tita's memory—and love story—alive. But it's also apparent that their romance continues through her recipes passed down to the next generation. As long as Tita's ancestors continue to make her food and infuse their own love and passion into them, Tita and Pedro will live on and get the happy ending they were denied in life.

Esquivel's novel was published during a push to bring attention to the work of ignored minority female writers and a celebration of multicultural literature. Her book was championed alongside works like Gabriel García Márquez's *Love in the Time of Cholera* and Isabel Allende's *House of the Spirits*. The adaptation of *Like Water for Chocolate* went on to become the highest-grossing foreign language film ever released in the United States at that time, and was Mexico's entry for the Academy Awards, though, sadly, it was not nominated. Esquivel wrote two additional installments of Tita's journey: She published *Tita's Diary* in 2016 and *The Colors of My Past* in 2017, focusing on a relative of Tita's discovering her diary.

THE BRIDGES OF MADISON COUNTY

1995

Directed by Clint Eastwood
Screenplay by Richard LaGravenese
Based on *The Bridges of Madison County*
by Robert James Waller, 1992

"This kind of certainty comes but just once in a lifetime."

Robert James Waller's 1992 romantic novel *The Bridges of Madison County* is a tale of dreams deferred and what happens when two middle-aged people at different points in their life find love. The novel tells the story of Francesca Johnson (Meryl Streep), an Italian war bride, wife, and mother to two teenage children. Over a four-day period in 1965 she meets *National Geographic* photographer Robert Kincaid (Clint Eastwood), who is photographing all the covered bridges in the county. The two quickly fall in love but, with Francesca's family set to return home from a 4-H trip, she must decide whether to give up the life she's known for this newfound romance.

The Bridges of Madison County garnered attention even before its publication. Director Steven Spielberg and his production company, Amblin Entertainment, purchased the rights to Waller's novel in 1991, a year before it hit shelves, for $25,000. The plan was for Spielberg to direct but when he was unable to, he looked to various directors, including Sydney Pollack—who wanted to reunite with his *Out of Africa* star Robert Redford and screenwriter Kurt Ludetke—as well as Bruce Beresford, of *Driving Miss Daisy* (1989) fame. Clint Eastwood was attached from the beginning to play Robert Kincaid, and when he clashed with Beresford and caused the director to walk away from the project, Eastwood took over and brought Meryl Streep on board.

Screenwriter Richard LaGravenese crafted a framing device exclusive to the movie featuring Francesca's adult children returning to the Iowa farmhouse of their youth to settle their mother's estate. They're surprised to discover she wants to be cremated and her ashes scattered from the Roseman Covered Bridge, a location whose meaning is lost on them. While going through her effects, the kids discover a diary in which she documents her affair with Kincaid.

The novel holds much in common with Noel Coward's 1934 play *Still Life*, itself the foundation for the 1945 feature *Brief Encounter*. Like *Bridges*, the story follows a married woman and a single man who try to figure out if they can make a relationship work. But Waller also borrows from Alexandre Dumas's *Camille*, in that an unnamed narrator—potentially Waller himself—tells the story at the request of Francesca's children. (In the movie, the kids narrate by reading the diary in Francesca's voice.) The book narrator decides to turn the story into a book itself, fleshing out Francesca and Robert's characters as the result of his "research" on them. This device gives additional backstory, such as Robert's upbringing: He's described as a loner with no close friends, both parents dead, and no connection to other relatives. His ex-wife, Marian, is said to have left him nine years earlier after five years of marriage. The book also expands on Francesca's girlhood and time as an Italian war bride.

The novel's framework lends an air of legitimacy, creating a story that could happen to anyone, and is so poignant that the narrator said it "reduced my level of cynicism about what is possible in the arena of human relationships." Waller's novel is incredibly philosophical and florid in style, something that initially turned Streep off of the project until Eastwood promised her that LaGravenese's script would eliminate all that. Waller's words are beautiful, and emphasize the spirituality and

sensuality that exists between Francesca and Robert from their first meeting. The slightest interaction between them is imbued with erotic meaning, intensifying their relationship before it ever becomes physical. This flowery writing can make the characters come off more like gods than humans, especially Robert, who is described by numerous people in the book, including his own mother, as being "not of this Earth," ethereal and spectral. Francesca describes him as animal-like, a "leopard riding on the tail of a comet." The movie simplifies everything and gives us Robert and Francesca as just two people, with nothing special or otherworldly about them.

Since the novel is sold as a "true" story or biography, there is no central protagonist. The narrator/author controls how the story plays out. The novel opens with Robert's story, then vacillates between his and Francesca's. Eastwood told Streep that the story would be from Francesca's point of view, making the central conflict her desire to run off with Robert or stay with her family. Eastwood also made the decision to film the movie in chronological order, laid out like the book. This choice wasn't to mimic the novel but to enhance the power of his and Streep's performance. "We were two people getting to know each other, in real time, as actors and characters." Robert is still a dream man, but making Francesca the central character in the movie means she sees how he's ideal yet also allows her to question the reality of how little she knows him. The author admits that much of Robert's life after leaving Francesca is unknown. An epilogue includes an interview with fictional jazz musician Nighthawk Cummings to fill in the gaps.

In the book, Francesca worries what people in the town would say about seeing a strange man's car in her driveway, so after moving the car the couple's relationship is confined to inside her house. Through the book Francesca worries about how people would react to her leaving her husband and children. The town of Redfern is shown to be one that doesn't take kindly to any change, the townsfolk gossiping about Robert's hippie style (his long hair and penchant for bracelets and sandals) as he eats in a local diner. The fear of being condemned by them isn't a concern for Francesca on-screen—she worries more about what her family will think—but Robert witnesses the town's reaction to alleged cheaters while eating in the local diner. Everyone in the room suddenly goes quiet when Lucy Redfield (Michelle Benes), the mistress of a local man, enters.

The pair have an intense relationship over the span of the weekend, but Francesca is at odds over whether to abandon her children and her husband, a man who has stayed loyal to her. She is also afraid the intensity of her relationship with Robert will flame out. Each iteration of the story ends with Francesca deciding to stay with her family and questioning whether she made the right decision. As famously detailed in the movie, Francesca waits in the car for her husband when she sees Robert, standing out in the rain. Later, Francesca and her husband are driving behind Robert. He puts on his blinker, indicating to Francesca she still has an opportunity to go with him, which she refuses. The book closes Francesca's story on a bittersweet note. Francesca dies at the age of sixty-nine, with the doctors finding her death mysterious because "we can find no specific cause . . ." Whether Francesca died of a broken heart or because of her desperation to be reunited with Robert, the spiritual nature of Waller's story illustrates love's ability to transcend death itself.

By the time the film version of *The Bridges of Madison County* hit theaters the book had already sold 9.5 million copies, with many comparing it to Erich Segal's *Love Story*. The book stayed on the *New York Times* Best Sellers list for the next three years.

WAITING TO EXHALE

1995

Directed by Forest Whitaker
Screenplay by Terry McMillan and Ron Bass
Based on *Waiting to Exhale* by Terry McMillan, 1992

"The deal is, the men in Denver are dead."

The classic romance model is one where a couple find each other, each possessing traits that complement the other, on their way to a happily ever after. But as Terry McMillan lays out in her 1992 novel *Waiting to Exhale*, it's next to impossible to find Prince Charming in this modern day and age. Set in 1990, *Waiting to Exhale* tells the story of four friends, all professional Black women, trying to find love and respect in Phoenix, Arizona. From career woman Savannah (Whitney Houston) and wealthy housewife Bernadine (Angela Bassett) to the boy crazy Robin (Lela Rochon) and single mother Gloria (Loretta Devine), each goes through a series of trials and romantic entanglements on their way to finding self-empowerment. All the way, their friendships remain strong.

The book plays on several themes previously established in McMillan's 1989 novel *Disappearing Acts*, which looked at doomed romantic relationships between Black couples.

McMillan's novel skirts the line between being a romance novel and a dramatic one. It isn't that the four women lack relationships and sex—with the exception of Gloria, who unfortunately suffers from a lot of 1990s-era fat shaming, which is cited as the reason she's single. It's that the women struggle to find men who can offer them the security they need to be themselves.

The central premise of each woman's plot is how romance affects her, with an added element of striving to find self-worth. Whether the four women end up in a relationship or not is less important by the end than how they stay together in tough times and learn to appreciate themselves. But each of the women think they can't find a quality man. Some of the relationships they have throughout the book are with married men, men who do drugs, men who prefer to date white women, and men who just can't commit for one reason or another. McMillan weaves this in with other issues affecting the Black community during the early 1990s, from the rising crack cocaine epidemic to the challenge of making Martin Luther King Jr. Day a holiday in the state of Arizona (which officially passed the year of the book's release).

When director Forest Whitaker and co-screenwriter Ron Bass turned *Waiting to Exhale* into a movie, much of the novel's social commentary was removed to focus on the individual romantic relationships plus the women's overarching friendship. Robin's boyfriend Troy (Mykelti Williamson) smoking and dealing crack and the group's Black Women on the Move meetings—an organization empowering Black women to help their communities—are eliminated. Because of this change, each woman's individual problems unrelated to their romantic partners are nixed, like Robin's financial issues as she tries to pay her student loans while coping with her father's Alzheimer's diagnosis.

Another excised subplot focuses on how Gloria became pregnant with her son, Tarik (Donald Faison) during her first year of college; she refuses to have an abortion because of her Catholic upbringing. Her boyfriend, David (Giancarlo Esposito), is a track-and-field star going to the Olympics, so Gloria says if he only acknowledges the child she'll be happy, as she doesn't want to ruin his future. Bernadine regularly visits her mother, a former school bus driver, in the book, while Savannah has a sister and two brothers, one of whom is in the military and another in jail.

Both the book and movie highlight the flaws of Black men, but the women are not immune from having flaws of their own, though the book shows the dated thought process of the times regarding female autonomy. Because the book gives insight into the women's states of mind, the reader hears how they each think about one another. In the book, Robin—lovingly called "the whore" by her friends—tells Savannah that she won't eat alone in a restaurant as she refuses to be judged for not having a man. Savannah grows irritated with her and thinks to herself, "Women like [Robin] really piss me off." For Savannah, Robin is vain and helpless without a man.

Bernadine, Robin, and Savannah routinely bring up Gloria's weight and how much prettier she'd be—and more enticing to men—if she lost a few pounds. This plotline becomes crueler once Gloria has a massive heart attack (in the book, not the film), with Bernadine joking to Gloria that it's an extreme way for her to go on a diet. Gloria's eventual relationship with next-door neighbor Marvin (Gregory Hines) is darling. Marvin's love for Gloria is just as strong in the book. After Gloria's heart attack, he tells the nurse he's her husband so he can stay with her. The movie still has Gloria labeled as the chubby friend but it's presented more as how she views herself. Her friends don't validate it. Because the other friends' commentary isn't present, the audience understands Gloria believes her weight is an impediment when it really isn't.

Bernadine sees the biggest change between page and film, but that doesn't diminish Bassett's performance—including her iconic walk away from the burning car she's just lit on fire containing her husband's stuff. Bernadine's relationship with her husband John (Michael Beach) is said to have been over for years in the novel, but neither one of them has verbalized it. The movie streamlines her plot to focus on how she raises her two children in the wake of a nasty court case wherein John is hiding his money. At the end of the film, John and Bernadine come to accept that their marriage is over and walk away from each other as amicably as they can. In the book, Bernadine spends more time wallowing in bitterness upon hearing John wants to marry his mistress, Kathleen (Kelly Preston).

Bernadine can seem crueler in the book than in the film, but it stems from her feelings of failure, fear of losing her husband, and thinking she's not enough. She leaves the kids with her mother and does nothing, not even brushing her teeth, for four days. When she hears that her children went to her husband's wedding, and that Kathleen is pregnant, she freaks out.

She eventually meets a man named James (Wesley Snipes), who is married to a white woman dying of cancer. James is the ideal man in the movie, one so in love and devoted to his wife that although he has a connection with Bernadine, he refuses to pursue it. The book explains that James and his wife are on the verge of divorce because his wife didn't want children. James and Bernadine sleep together, with James saying she's "restored my faith in Black women," and the pair are together at the novel's climax, with Bernadine revealing herself to be a millionaire due to a prodigious court settlement.

Terry McMillan remains one of the foremost Black authors and later chronicled the further adventures of her *Exhale* characters in the 2010 sequel novel *Getting to Happy*. While the novel's themes are dated, they are a window into the 1990s landscape Black women faced regarding their identities and what they were looking for in men and relationships.

THE PORTRAIT OF A LADY

1996

Directed by Jane Campion
Screenplay by Laura Jones
Based on *The Portrait of a Lady* by Henry James, 1881

"I love you, but without hope."

Author Henry James was one of the most prolific American authors of his time. In the four decades in which he was writing he published more than one hundred novels, including what many critics call his masterpiece: *The Portrait of a Lady*. The novel follows Isabel Archer (Nicole Kidman in the film), an American expatriate who travels throughout Europe on a quest for identity and autonomy.

Hollywood started adapting James's work in 1933 with *Berkeley Square*. The most famous adaptation, thanks to an Oscar-winning performance by Olivia de Havilland, is 1949's *The Heiress*, an adaptation of James's 1880 novel *Washington Square*. It's said that producer David O. Selznick wanted to adapt *The Portrait of a Lady* in the 1950s with his wife Jennifer Jones as Isabel Archer. The possible delay in bringing the book to the big screen lies in the various themes James navigates within it, particularly the class and social differences between European aristocracy and American aristocracy. The novel, on the surface, is about one woman's pressure to marry and her desire to resist it, but James uses that to explore individualism and how it conflicts with social customs. In James's examination of the dynamics between America and Europe, the various people Isabel encounters, from her best friend Henrietta Stackpole (Mary-Louise Parker) to Isabel's cousin Ralph (Martin Donovan), want her to cement an identity (as either an American or a European) through matrimony. Isabel finds herself drawn to the mysterious American-born, European-raised Gilbert Osmond (John Malkovich), who convinces Isabel to put aside her wayward lifestyle for marriage. But in marrying Gilbert, Isabel discovers she will not be able to have everything she wants in life. James himself was an American-born author whose books looked at the social movements of the upper class, particularly American expatriates living in England, but that's writ large in *The Portrait of a Lady.*

Isabel comes to represent the innocence and optimism of America at the time butting against the decadent social sophistication and restriction found within Europe. For as much as Isabel Archer touts her desire to be free and do what she wants, she also desperately wants the safety and stability marriage offers women. For all her friends' love, they question her complete loyalty to them (and the countries they represent) through her relationships. Henrietta Stackpole specifically mentions wanting Isabel to marry the kind yet intimidating Caspar Goodwood (Viggo Mortensen). To her friends, marriage is a literal alignment of individuals, a quasi–business relationship, and whomever Isabel marries will show whether she aligns with optimistic America or the old guard that is England. (James himself became a naturalized British citizen in 1915—and lived there until his death the following year—in protest against America's failure to enter World War I.) For Isabel, love isn't just about romance, but social stability and financial security. To her friends, an ideal alliance shows the ultimate love for her country.

In 1996, New Zealand director Jane Campion sought to tell Isabel Archer's story with Nicole Kidman in the title role. Screenwriter Laura Jones nixes much of the American versus European subtext to tell a straightforward story of Isabel's quest for independence and how her marriage to Osmond (John Malkovich) seeks to destroy that. In the movie Isabel's search for love compels her to choose between independence and autonomy, but Isabel is still extremely naive and Gilbert is purely out to use Isabel for her money and to control her. She falls for Gilbert out of a belief that he loves her, only to discover he's a monster.

By opening the movie with images of modern-day women, living portraits of femininity today, Campion expands and makes Isabel Archer a feminist character who inspires generations of women today. That being said, Isabel is a more thinly drawn character in the movie, potentially to reflect James's penchant for telling the story two ways: one through the eyes of peripheral characters in Isabel's life, and then through the character's own eyes.

In the book, Isabel is said to have had a close relationship with her father, who educated her in a liberal way that many, including her aunt Mrs. Touchett (Shelley Winters in the film), find scandalous. (The reader also learns about Isabel's two sisters, Edith and Lillian. Edith is described as the prettiest of the Archer siblings, Lillian the most sensible, and Isabel the most intelligent.) Because of her father's coddling, Isabel has a highly romanticized view of the world. She wants to pay her own way through Europe but doesn't realize she can't afford to, so Mrs. Touchett secretly pays for her, with Isabel unaware of her aunt's assistance. James's intent with Isabel, as a character, is to make the audience fascinated and frustrated with her. The novel jumps forward in several-year intervals throughout Isabel's life, with James not always content to fill the reader in on what has happened in between these flash-forwards. James called this technique "elliptical storytelling," skipping over important incidents or implying crucial events in the aftermath of their occurrence. James uses elliptical storytelling in moments when Isabel is going to make a decision that favors social convention over her own independence, such as marrying Gilbert Osmond.

And while both the novel and film focus on Isabel's relationship with Osmond, both versions also feature another subplot wherein Isabel's friend Henrietta (Mary-Louise Parker) engages in a companionship and marriage with a man named Mr. Bantling. This plot point is particularly important to the book, as Henrietta prides herself on being a strong-headed feminist. Isabel ends up disappointed to discover that even Henrietta has fallen back on social convention and gotten married.

The book and movie put Isabel in very different places by the end. The movie culminates with the death of Isabel's cousin Ralph (Martin Donovan), and Isabel deciding whether she will go home to Osmond or not. Is she going to stick to convention and keep to her "duty" to stay married, or will she shatter the trend and live life as a divorced woman? The film ends ambiguously, with Isabel looking into the camera, her fate left to be decided by the viewer.

The novel ends with Isabel returning to Rome, back to her passionless marriage with Osmond and her desire to continue to lust for security while hating her confinement. At the end, Henrietta and Isabel's scorned suitor Caspar Goodwood (Viggo Mortensen) stand together, walking back to their American ideals. Isabel goes off into the ether, with the reader having no idea what her fate will be, yet knowing that she has lost something.

Neither movie nor book is particularly hopeful or romantic, but the point of both is to show how people romanticize and idealize others. Sometimes those idealizations bear fruit, and sometimes they fall short. Regardless, Isabel Archer remains such an enigmatic character that each reminds us she'll never truly be forgotten.

THE ENGLISH PATIENT

1996

Directed by Anthony Minghella
Screenplay by Anthony Minghella
Based on *The English Patient* by Michael Ondaatje, 1992

"Every night I cut out my heart. But in the morning it was full again."

Sri Lankan poet-turned-author Michael Ondaatje's 1992 novel *The English Patient* is a lyrical, highly detailed exploration of love across the decades and how its sacred qualities overcome time and geography. Written in a fragmented, poetic style by Ondaatje, the novel tells the story of a World War II nurse named Hana (Juliette Binoche in the movie) caring for a severely burned man (Ralph Fiennes) suffering from amnesia. With the help of a thief who has lost his thumbs, named Caravaggio (Willem Dafoe), and a Sikh bomb expert (Naveen Andrews), the trio learn about the burned man, dubbed "the English patient," and his past, which includes an affair with the beautiful and wealthy Katharine Clifton (Kristin Scott Thomas).

Because of Ondaatje's specific writing style, director Anthony Minghella found the task of adapting the novel daunting. "Its gifts, in a way, are very elusive and are very much connected with the beauty of language, which is probably the thing that the film is least good at conveying." Ondaatje worked on the script with Minghella, sharing the belief that most people seeing the movie never read the book in the first place. The book's events happen over several years, and rather than focus on complex themes of national identity and the fluid connections between time and history, it made more sense for the movie to situate the love story between the English patient and Katharine as the primary narrative, with a parallel romance between nurse Hana and bomb expert Kip.

The film parcels out the mystery of the English patient's identity over a near three-hour run time, whereas the book has no chronological structure and alternates between the past and the present, telling the patient's story backward. The reader is an outside observer and learns about things in a realistic manner. No one can predict when a life-changing moment will happen in their lives and the same goes for Hana, the patient, and everyone else. Information is given to them and it takes several chapters for the reader, and the character, to understand the significance of that information.

Ondaatje, a Sri Lankan man living in Canada, makes multiculturalism and the history of exoticizing the desert key themes in *The English Patient*. This is evident in the depiction of Kip, a Sikh man finding his way in the English world of colonialism. In the book, Kip loves the English and the West, so much so that he sings their songs and wears their clothes. The movie touches on these themes here and there, but in the book Kip is, at times, more important than the English patient himself.

Unlike the movie, where Kip meets Hana as he tries to defuse a minefield on the road she's traveling, the novel shows him accidentally stumble upon her playing the piano at the villa where she's been holed up since the novel's first page. As the two grow closer, he tells her about his family and how he was expected to become a doctor but instead decided to enter the army and, through the mentorship of Lord Suffolk (a real-life person), became a bomb expert.

Several chapters are devoted to Kip's stories of defusing bombs and saving English lives, all aided by Lord Suffolk's encouragement. As Kip says, Lord Suffolk is the first person to treat him like a fellow Englishman and not a foreigner. However, when the atomic bomb is dropped on Hiroshima—illustrating how much time passes in the book compared to the movie—Kip becomes so wild with rage that he plans to shoot the patient, believing the unnamed man represents every evil the English and the West have committed against Asia. Kip feels that if Japan were a white country, those in charge would not have been so hasty to drop the bomb. The patient welcomes death, but Kip can't pull the trigger. With the explosion of the atomic bomb, Kip's belief system is literally shattered, leaving him to find a new path in life that, sadly, doesn't include Hana.

Kip is such a large part of the narrative that the novel even ends on his character. The movie ends with Hana and Kip parting because his job takes him to other areas of the country. They agree to meet again, but Kip completely discards his Western life. Years pass and Kip becomes the doctor his family wanted him to be. He is married and has two children. He says he received letters from Hana for a year, but never responded to them.

This bittersweet ending is paralleled alongside the story of the patient and Katharine. The love affair between the English patient, revealed as Hungarian cartographer László Almásy, and Katharine Clifton is told on-screen similarly to how it presents on the page, albeit in chronological order and as the overarching story. The pair meet and engage in a powerfully

charged romance despite Katharine being married. Almásy and Katharine have a highly sexual affair with moments of extreme toxicity, trying to repel each other because of their awareness that outside forces are pulling them apart. Katharine takes her frustration out on Almásy in the novel by not only hitting him (also seen on screen), but throwing plates and stabbing him with forks. When people notice his plentiful bruises, Almásy makes up excuses, leading them to think he's a klutz.

The couple's affair is eventually discovered by Katharine's jealous husband, Geoffrey (Colin Firth), who has been spying on her. Geoffrey, accompanied by his wife in a biplane, travels to Cairo in order to kill his competition and commit a murder/suicide by crashing the airplane into the desert sand where Almásy, preparing to leave, is waiting. The crash kills Geoffrey and leaves Katharine severely wounded. Almásy shelters Katharine in a cave and goes off to get help, eventually evading arrest and stealing an airplane to rescue her.

Geoffrey is British Intelligence in the book and works as an aerial photographer. Because the intelligence agency knows of Almásy's affair with Katharine, they assume Geoffrey's death is suspicious and imprison Almásy as he tries to get help. His story then jumps ahead three months as he returns to the cave and finds Katharine dead. The movie shows this discovery as a tender moment, with only a few days passing and Almásy lying next to Katharine's recently deceased body, stroking her hair. The book is more macabre, with Almásy making love to Katharine's body, a final blending of life and death, love and sex, body and mind.

The English Patient was nominated for twelve Academy Awards and won nine, including Best Picture. The movie's sweeping visuals and romantic love story evoked a sentiment similar to 1940s war romances. It was highly praised upon release, though contemporary audiences today place the moment in the "when Oscar gets it wrong" category due to a perceived lack of staying power and quality compared to fellow nominee *Fargo* (1996). Regardless, Minghella's film is an utterly beautiful and romantic story, a daunting feat considering how equally beautiful, though different, its source material is.

HOW STELLA GOT HER GROOVE BACK

1998

Directed by Kevin Rodney Sullivan
Screenplay by Terry McMillan and Ron Bass
Based on *How Stella Got Her Groove Back*
by Terry McMillan, 1996

"It's kind of getting on my nerves if you want the truth, listening to her go on and on about how she can't believe she's fallen in love with this young man from Jamaica that she met on vacation . . ."

Three years after Terry McMillan's novel *Waiting to Exhale* was translated for the screen, Hollywood returned to her work with another adaptation: *How Stella Got Her Groove Back*. Hoping lightning would strike twice, Twentieth Century Fox reassembled several key elements from *Exhale* for the movie, such as actress Angela Bassett and co-screenwriter Ron Bass.

The story follows successful stockbroker Stella Payne (Bassett), who, in a desire to shake up her life, takes a trip to Jamaica. Once there she meets and falls in love with the charming Winston (Taye Diggs), a man twenty-plus years her junior. As the pair start their newfound relationship, they have to deal with not only their age gap but cultural and personality differences as well.

While participating in a twenty-fifth anniversary panel for *Stella*, Bassett said that she appreciated McMillan's work because the author "ushered in this moment, through her books about Black women full of assuredness and [who] exist regardless of what society says."

McMillan focuses on how romance is one of numerous things women have to fit into the narrative of who they are as people. *How Stella Got Her Groove Back* is firmly a love story about two people who overcome differences of generation, class, and identity in order to take a risk on love. The book is also a story of how Stella finds her own identity as a forty-two-year-old woman on her way to raising a teenager. The book sees her question a future where her son grows up, and where she's forced to change her job and start all over in a new career. Stella believes she's a one-woman show, content to do everything on her own, even go on a vacation to a foreign country. Winston's arrival in her life not only makes her wonder whether she can be the paramour of a twenty-year-old man, but if she is willing to give up living and being alone.

Stella is the prism through which everything revolves. In the book, she is our narrator and the only person the reader knows with any sense of intimacy. Stella has few friends, one of them a gallery owner named Maisha who wants Stella to take up art. When Stella is in Jamaica she spends time with random hotel guests, particularly a newlywed couple from Canada named Ben and Sasha. The movie understands that Stella can't talk exclusively in voiceover nor confess her deepest thoughts to random characters, so it expands the role of her friend Delilah (Whoopi Goldberg), whom Stella mentions in the book recently died of cancer. In the film, Delilah battles cancer in secret and is the one who compels Stella to go on the trip . . . and bring her along. Stella finds out about the cancer a week before Delilah dies in the book. The two experience Jamaica side by side, with Stella able to discuss her hopes and fears about love and life with someone close to her. Halfway through the movie, Stella must become a source of strength for Delilah before her death.

As with *Waiting to Exhale*, McMillan explores issues that affect Black people of the time. As Stella travels through Jamaica, she notices both the acceptance of Black people and the economic disparity between those living on the island and Black people in America. "The one thing I can't help but notice is that everybody here is Black," Stella says, surprised at not being the minority in the country.

Stella starts to look at everything in Jamaica through the lens of American racism. When Stella takes a horseback ride away from the resort, she notices the poor, working-class Jamaicans who live in shantytowns who remind her of her own grandparents who lived in the South. Visiting a nude beach, Stella decides to do like everyone else and take her clothes off, which causes her to become conscious of how white people stare at her body on the beach, extrapolating it as how they look at her in society. Stella doesn't interpret this as having anything to do with her beauty but rather with ownership of

Black female bodies during slave times, so her moment on the beach is a reclamation of her person.

Stella's interiority is also a reason why most of her relationship with Winston is changed for the movie. The film plays it as a straightforward generational divide. Winston and Stella spend their time in Jamaica getting to know each other—Stella even meets his parents, who think she is too old for him—before Winston visits her in California. Once there, the movie's second half deals with Stella's family and her ex-husband meeting Winston, as well as Stella's own hangups about living with another person, let alone a younger man from a different culture. The book explores the economic divide between Stella and Winston, particularly once Winston makes the leap to visit Stella in America. He's impressed by how large her house is, which she finds odd. She thinks it's average. These issues show the various obstacles, both personal and societal, the pair have to overcome if they want to stay together.

Winston, at just twenty years old, is depicted as knowing what he wants in a relationship and is underestimated by Stella. However, there is still a harsh level of naivety written into him as he admits he's lived with his parents until recently and has just secured his first job ever. We don't know anything about Winston's life when he isn't with Stella, leaving her to perpetually fall into rages when she can't get ahold of him, fearing that he's moved on and is no longer interested in her.

Stella is still the one trying to suss out how she feels about the relationship once he arrives in California. This culminates in an argument between the couple in which Stella points out Winston's immaturity while he brings up how controlling she is. When Winston proposes toward the book's end, Stella has to decide if she's willing to take a risk, not knowing if their relationship is going to last or not.

The movie concludes with the standard happy ending. The two part, before eventually reconciling as he's about to board a plane back home. Though we don't know what happens in the next scene, Hollywood filmmaking implies Winston and Stella live happily ever after. McMillan ends her book on an ambiguous note. Will Stella and Winston make it to the altar? Will he eventually outgrow her? The reader doesn't know because reality doesn't work that way. All they can do is take Stella and Winston's love on faith and pray for the best, much like they would if this was real life.

The legacy of *How Stella Got Her Groove Back* manifests in unexpected ways today: Stella's fantastic wardrobe in the movie comes courtesy of costume designer Ruth E. Carter, who went on to become the first Black woman and first African American ever to win the Academy Award for Best Costumes, for her work on the 2018 film *Black Panther*, also starring Angela Bassett.

OUT OF SIGHT

1998

Directed by Steven Soderbergh
Screenplay by Scott Frank
Based on *Out of Sight* by Elmore Leonard, 1996

"You'd be surprised about what you can get, if you ask for it the right way."

Two people, a man and a woman, lie side by side in the trunk of a car. The man is a criminal and the woman is the federal agent he's kidnapped. There's little fear in their interaction, however. The pair discuss movies and, while talking about their love for Faye Dunaway in *Three Days of the Condor* (1975), a romance blossoms. This is the central dynamic between US federal marshal Karen Sisco (Jennifer Lopez) and slick bank robber Jack Foley (George Clooney) in Elmore Leonard's 1996 novel *Out of Sight*. As the two play a game of cat and mouse, Foley and Sisco can't deny their attraction to each other, which causes each of them to break the rules when it comes to their respective businesses.

Movies have played up the sexy fun of breaking the law from 1932's *Trouble in Paradise* to 1968's *Thomas Crown Affair*. But the crackling dialogue and drawn-out eroticism of Steven Soderbergh's adaptation of Leonard's novel takes it to another level. From the moment Jack and Karen find themselves together in the trunk of her car after Jack escapes from prison, Soderbergh and Leonard make a point of saying these two have an undeniable chemistry. Jack says, in both the book and the film, that he's curious about what would happen if they met under different circumstances. After that, the pair constantly try to answer that question together. There's an Old Hollywood sensuousness to their missed encounters. A moment when Karen sees Jack in an elevator draws comparisons to Cary Grant and Irene Dunne in 1940's *My Favorite Wife*. The audience isn't necessarily interested in these two going to bed—though Soderbergh's camera beautifully captures that scene—but rather how these two are going to find a way to make it work between them.

What's unique about Leonard's book is how it tells a straightforward crime thriller with occasional levity. Soderbergh, as he did with his remake of *Ocean's Eleven*, makes a crime-comedy where the characters are light and funny while committing crimes. Striking that balance in Soderbergh's film allows the romance between Karen and Foley to feel organic. Leonard's more serious book makes the romance a respite from all the darkness they experience. Karen is committed to bringing Foley in, yet she provides him with numerous opportunities to escape. The reader learns how Karen was in a similar situation with a previous boyfriend, a man named Carl Tillman, who was also a bank robber. Though "when the time came," Karen shot (and presumably killed) him. Is this Karen's kink? Karen says she wasn't aware he was a criminal, but it's never definitively proven. The relationships are further paralleled in the book's finale, where Karen is forced to decide if she's going to shoot Jack or not.

Screenwriter Scott Frank streamlined the story, softening the darker parts of Leonard's novel to make it more comedic.

The movie's narrative jumps backward and forward in time, starting with Foley's jailbreak and then going back to how he ended up there, whereas Leonard writes the story in chronological order, starting with Foley's escape and Karen hunting him from Miami to Detroit. In the movie, Foley's motivation to escape is to simultaneously get revenge on Richard Ripley (Albert Brooks), a white-collar criminal he knew in prison who claims to have diamonds in his house, as well as secure a substantial amount in loot. Foley and Buddy team up with violent boxer Maurice "Snoopy" Miller (Don Cheadle) to pull off the heist. The Ripley heist is what everyone works toward in the movie, but in the book it's merely where the finale takes place. Ripley is nothing more than a name in the book—he isn't even home when the group gets to his house.

Alongside Jackie Brown, the heroine of the 1992 novel *Rum Punch*, Karen Sisco is one of Leonard's best remembered heroines. Leonard was inspired to write the character after seeing a photo in the *Detroit News* of a federal marshal holding a shotgun on her hip. This photo is mimicked in the book and in the film as well. Foley hopes to find out where Karen is staying in Detroit and randomly looks at a newspaper, seeing Karen in that same pose. Much of Karen's dialogue is also lifted directly from the book.

Sandra Bullock was initially cast in the role but was replaced after Soderbergh said she and Clooney failed to have romantic chemistry. "It was not Elmore Leonard energy," Clooney said in a 1998 interview. Interestingly, neither Lopez nor Bullock fits the description of Karen in the book, where Leonard portrays her as a sexy blonde.

Leonard ends his book with a wink. Karen turns Jack in and, during a talk with her father, Marshall (Dennis Farina), gets the idea to fly with Foley back to prison. The flight offers one more romantic interlude together, and who knows what might happen? Foley's fate remains unknown. The movie gives a more definitive ending, with Karen driving Jack back to prison and bringing along another prisoner for transport, Hejira Henry (Samuel L. Jackson), who is a multiple escapee like Foley. As Karen smiles, the audience understands that it's only a matter of time before she's chasing Foley again.

Leonard's novels have been consistently adapted since 1957's dual releases of *3:10 to Yuma* and *The Tall T*. But just a year prior to the release of *Out of Sight*, Quentin Tarantino directed his version of *Rum Punch*, entitled *Jackie Brown*. The movie is a Tarantino crime thriller, though it has a "love on the run" narrative between Pam Grier's Jackie and Robert Forster's Max Cherry, similar to *Out of Sight*. Michael Keaton, who plays DEA agent Ray Nicolette in *Jackie Brown*, reprises the character in *Out of Sight*, one of the few characters lifted directly and unaltered from Leonard's book.

Crime doesn't pay, but it certainly looks sexy. Both versions of *Out of Sight* make a point of that. Leonard's work is darker than Soderbergh's slick heist film, but the romance shines through no matter which version you're spending time with.

CHOCOLAT

2000

Directed by Lasse Hallstrom
Screenplay by Robert Nelson Jacobs
Based on *Chocolat* by Joanne Harris, 1999

"So, through good times and bad, famine and feast, the villagers held fast to their traditions. Until, one winter day, a sly wind blew in from the North . . ."

Some books (and movies) make you hungry, and much like love itself, sometimes that hunger can be insatiable. Joanne Harris's 1999 novel, *Chocolat*, adapted for the screen in 2000 by director Lasse Hallström, explores the connection between love and food. The novel tells the story of the nomadic Vianne Rocher (Juliette Binoche), who moves to the stodgy French town of Lansquenet-sous-Tannes with her six-year-old daughter Anouk (Victoire Thivisol). The townsfolk do little outside of going to church, where they're constantly judged, and they live in fear of the local priest, Francis Reynaud (Alfred Molina). Anything, or anyone, perceived as unsavory or out of the ordinary is cast out. Vianne is determined to make Lansquenet her home and opens a chocolaterie called La Celeste Praline. But as Vianne becomes more popular with her neighbors, Reynaud starts to see her as a negative influence and is determined to destroy her business for good.

Chocolat uses sweets and magical realism to explore deep-seated themes like the nature of faith, guilt, and tolerance. Vianne and her late mother are described as witches (though Vianne doesn't like the term) who engage in "chocolate scrying" to see people's inner thoughts and desires. Vianne and Anouk have a near-psychic bond, and the young girl appears to have inherited her mother's powers. She communicates with an imaginary rabbit named Pantoufle, whom Vianne sometimes sees. (The film changes Pantoufle to a kangaroo.) The film is more lighthearted, presenting Vianne's powers as metaphorical rather than literal. The scrying is still in the film but is used to help Vianne determine a person's favorite chocolate. The various chocolates Vianne gives out do have magical qualities; some have aphrodisiac properties that help rekindle the love between a dowdy woman and her uninterested husband.

A brief backstory exclusive to the movie is depicted, in which Vianne's father travels to Central America to study the holistic properties of chocolate. He falls in love with a local woman, Chitza, Vianne's mother. Chitza eventually takes Vianne and leaves her husband, putting them on the wandering path that Vianne continues with Anouk today.

Harris's book is less a novel of romantic love than it is about a mother's love for her child. It also illustrates the power of community and how food creates memories. Binoche's performance garnered her a Best Actress nomination, and her Vianne is sensual and exuberant. In the book, Vianne wrestles with inner guilt over her mother's death from cancer and is determined not to give Anouk the same nomadic lifestyle she had growing up. Vianne's work is meant to leave a legacy, not only for Anouk, but for everyone in the town. Through the chocolaterie, Vianne brings together the townspeople, as well as fellow outsiders, to create a makeshift family.

Vianne's story in the film is focused on the town being afraid to go outside the norm. As the narrator says, "If you lived in this village, you understood what was expected of you. You knew your place in the scheme of things. And if you happened to forget, someone would help remind you." The novel is darker, with Reynaud illustrating not only religious intolerance but Vianne's fear of "The Black Man," a mythical, devil-like character from her mother's folkloric stories that tried to separate mother and daughter when Vianne was younger.

Because Vianne is an outsider, as well as an unmarried woman with a child, Reynaud thinks she has an alchemical hold on everyone. Alfred Molina's interpretation of the Comte de Reynaud is not overtly malicious or frightening, but the character is more sinister on the page: The priest sees Vianne as a witch and believes it's his job to cleanse the town of vice. His narration is spoken to his former priest, who lives in a vegetative state after two strokes.

One of Vianne's allies in the book is the Irish-accented Roux (Johnny Depp), a red-headed, gregarious member of a Romani river brigade whose boat makes port in Lansquenet. Roux and the other Romani pirates are tormented by Reynaud and those who believe they bring trouble with them. He becomes a love interest for Vianne, a fellow nomad whom she finds herself drawn to. The movie portrays them as having much in common. They're both unjustly persecuted and seek to enjoy life. Because Vianne isn't outright looking for a partner in the book, she isn't upset when Roux falls for Vianne's friend Josephine Muscat (Lena Olin). Josephine has fled an abusive marriage and is trying to discover what actual love looks like, which she finds with Roux. Josephine becomes an independent woman who, in the film, is happy to stand on her own without a paramour.

Though Roux and Josephine are said to be a great fit, he and Vianne end up sleeping together. It's a moment of pure passion between the two, though Harris leaves it vague as to whether they love each other as anything more than friends. They're simply focused on living in the moment and appreciating the beauty of what's around them. Vianne discovers at the end of the book that she's pregnant, though it's unclear whether she and Roux will raise the child together. The movie ends with Roux, still a traveler at heart, telling Vianne that he is leaving with his Romani friends, but he plans to come back. A grown-up Anouk, revealed as the film's narrator, shares that Roux keeps his promise, returning to his love Vianne when summer arrives.

Chocolat was nominated for five Oscars, including Best Picture. Harris also brought back the characters for various sequels, starting with *The Girl with No Shadow* in 2007. That would be followed by the book *Peaches for Father Francis* in 2012 and *The Strawberry Thief* in 2019.

The book is a more serious work of magical realism and more limited in its romance, but it showcases a love affair with food, family, children, and community as opposed to one romantic prospect. In a sense, the book and film appease the same audience in different ways. The movie has a light and romantic mien, the milk chocolate of cinema if you will, while the book is pure dark chocolate. Both are utterly delicious.

BRIDGET JONES'S DIARY

2001

Directed by Sharon Maguire
Screenplay by Helen Fielding, Andrew Davies, and Richard Curtis
Based on *Bridget Jones's Diary* by Helen Fielding, 1996

"No, I like you very much. Just as you are."

Some romantic literature is a product of its environment, for good and ill. Such is the case with Helen Fielding's 1996 novel *Bridget Jones's Diary* and its 2001 adaptation. Inspired by Fielding's columns for the *Independent* and *The Daily Telegraph*, the story unfolds through the diary entries of Bridget Jones (Renée Zellweger), a thirtysomething single woman living in London. Bridget's personal and professional lives are messy. She bemoans what a nuisance her parents are, as well as the friends and colleagues who constantly remind her that she isn't married yet. Things become even messier once Bridget starts dating her boss, Daniel Cleaver (Hugh Grant), while simultaneously attracting the eye of Mark Darcy (Colin Firth), a successful lawyer and family friend.

Bridget Jones's Diary makes clear time and again that it's a 1990s novel. Bridget emphasizes that she should want a lover like Daniel to appreciate her for who she is, "but I am a child of *Cosmopolitan*." It is that *Cosmo* culture that leaves the novel out of touch at times. Bridget starts every chapter by listing her weight and the calories she's consumed (the movie introduces Bridget as being 132 pounds at the start; 129 in the book). Numerous comments are lobbed at Bridget or come up in her thoughts about her weight and her chronic fears of remaining single, which may make the book feel more mean-spirited to contemporary audiences.

Bridget Jones was a highly sought-after role regardless. Helena Bonham Carter, Cate Blanchett, and Cameron Diaz were considered at various points. Actress Rachel Weisz was deemed too beautiful for the part, while a post-*Titanic* Kate Winslet, at the age of twenty-four, was considered too young.

Fielding is a contrast to another popular female author, Candace Bushnell, who in 1994 started a series of columns for *The New York Observer* entitled *Sex and the City*. These columns served as inspiration for the popular HBO series, which premiered in 1998. Unlike Carrie Bradshaw, *Sex and the City*'s heroine, *Bridget Jones* is more focused on creating a relatable, complicated heroine trying to follow the trends aspirational characters like Carrie portray on-screen.

Aside from the characters, little of the plot was brought over from the pages of *Bridget Jones* to its big-screen version, even though author Helen Fielding is one of the screenwriters. The screenplay streamlines things into a love triangle between Bridget, Mark, and Daniel, excising Bridget's attempt to change to a career in broadcast journalism and her numerous sit-downs with her friends and their individual romantic entanglements, making Bridget's world smaller in the film than on the page. Bridget must choose between Mark and Daniel while also navigating the men's feud throughout the movie; Daniel tells Bridget that Mark slept with Daniel's fiancée, which ends up being untrue.

Both versions of Bridget have some growing up to do. She has a complicated, awkward, and at times embarrassing life in the movie, but the script cleans her up significantly compared to the novel, where Bridget spends her time complaining, counting calories, and drunkenly trying to write passages in her diary. By the end of the movie she realizes that, while Daniel is gorgeous and charming, she wants a man who loves her for who she is, flaws and all, which is Mark. Both versions are about finding someone who loves you warts and all, but in the film Bridget grows more as the result of her own inner desire to not be reliant on men, whereas in the book Bridget is more consumed with finding a man, and everything that happens in her life—her job, friends, and family—are a means of attaining that.

There are numerous allusions to Jane Austen's *Pride and Prejudice* peppered throughout Fielding's book, from Bridget's love/hate romance with Mark (his last name is Darcy, after all) to a scene where Bridget and her friends watch the premiere of the BBC's *Pride and Prejudice*, which later inspires Bridget to pitch a story to the entertainment television show she works for about its stars, Colin Firth and Jennifer Ehle. (It was this bit of meta cheek that enticed Firth into playing the role of Mark Darcy for the movie.)

Whereas the movie balances Mark and Daniel as opponents for Bridget's heart, the book's first half is very Daniel-focused. Mark pops up here and there but is more of an afterthought since Bridget is documenting what's happening in the moment. Once Mark enters Bridget's life, Daniel takes a sudden backseat. Daniel is written as a far more callous boyfriend. In the movie his engagement is presented to Bridget as a business merger, but in the book Daniel describes it as a whim. His relationship with Bridget concludes with a drunken phone call that makes her realize he'll never be there to support her. The fight sequence between Daniel and Mark that sets off the film's climax doesn't happen at all in the book, though it makes sense for the film, as it compels Bridget to make her own decision between the two men and gives the male actors necessary interaction.

The book's ending is a bit extra by comparison. A running subplot for Bridget is the dissolution of her parents' marriage. In the movie, her mother, Pamela (Gemma Jones), takes a job at a QVC-esque network and falls in love with one of the presenters. The relationship turns sour, causing Pamela to return home to her husband. In the book, Bridget's middle-aged mother leaves Bridget's dad to become a tabloid television reporter, which leads her to fall in love with a shady man named Julio (mimicking the Wickham/Lydia relationship in *Pride and Prejudice*). Eventually, Bridget learns that her mother and Julio have defrauded several family friends of their savings and fled to Portugal. Mark saves the day and brings Bridget's mom back home from Portugal while the authorities look for Julio. On Christmas day, Julio returns for Bridget's mother, culminating with Mark calling the police and putting Julio away for good. Mark then reveals his love for Bridget. Kooky as can be, but a very unexpected finale.

Bridget Jones continued her adventures with *Bridget Jones: The Edge of Reason* (1999), *Bridget Jones: Mad About the Boy* (2013), and *Bridget Jones's Baby* (2016). An adaptation of *Edge of Reason* hit theaters in 2004 and *Mad About the Boy* debuted on the Universal streaming app Peacock in 2025.

Bridget Jones's Diary is certainly one of those books and movies where "you had to be there" gets thrown around a lot. Regardless, each one is a frothy and engaging story about finding yourself and someone who loves you as you are.

THE NOTEBOOK

2004

Directed by Nick Cassavetes
Screenplay by Jeremy Leven
Based on *The Notebook* by Nicholas Sparks, 1996

"I want all of you,
forever.
You and me . . . everyday."

Nicholas Sparks's 1996 novel, adapted by Jeremy Leven for Nick Cassavetes in 2004, tells the story of two elderly people living in a nursing home, Duke (James Garner) and Allie (Gena Rowlands). The old man reads from a notebook to the woman every day, for reasons unknown. The notebook itself contains the story of poor working boy Noah (Ryan Gosling) and the wealthy Allie (Rachel McAdams), who meet in North Carolina in the summer of 1932 and fall into a heady romance. Allie leaves to go back home after the summer ends, and their relationship appears done for good. Years later, Allie returns to the town of New Bern to reunite with Noah before she marries successful lawyer Lon Hammond (James Marsden). The pair's reunion brings back all the old feelings, forcing Allie to decide which man she wants to spend her life with. All the while, the question remains of whose story Duke is reading. *The Notebook* is a story of remembrance and how the simple act of recollection keeps the spirit of love alive.

The Notebook became a *New York Times* bestseller in its first week of release and remained one for over a year. Hollywood wasted no time attempting an adaptation. In 1998, director Steven Spielberg wanted to direct it with Tom Cruise playing Noah. At one point, *My Left Foot* (1989) director Jim Sheridan was attached to the project, while at another, George Clooney was considered to play Noah with Paul Newman as Duke.

A nationwide casting search went out for the role of Allie when Cassavetes joined the project. Nearly every young actress at the time auditioned, including Jennifer Lawrence, Amy Adams, Claire Danes, and Reese Witherspoon. The choice allegedly came down to McAdams and singer Britney Spears, with McAdams walking away with the role.

Compared to the Cassavetes film, the book is vastly different in tone, narrative structure, and storytelling. Screenwriter Jeremy Leven's script moves the events from North Carolina to South Carolina and pushes the timeline of events up eight years to bring in World War II sooner and allow the characters to be high schoolers. Considering their youth in the movie, it makes more sense that Allie's parents believe she doesn't truly love Noah. In the book, Noah is already twenty-six by the time the war breaks out in 1941. (And although the lead actors play seventeen-year-olds in the film, Gosling was twenty-four when it debuted and McAdams was twenty-six.)

Noah and Allie's opening moments in the film are a highlight not found in the book, with a brash Noah so committed to getting a date from Allie that he hangs from the top of a Ferris Wheel and threatens to let go if she won't agree. Noah and Allie's courtship is only a few paragraphs in the book, with the pair meeting after graduation in 1932 at the Neuse River Festival. They spend several idyllic days together and lose their virginity to each other just three weeks before Allie leaves town.

The movie recounts events chronologically, whereas the book starts in the middle, with an adult Allie returning to the town of New Bern, North Carolina (Seabrook Island, South Carolina, in the movie), to find Noah after discovering he's bought his dream house—a house he promised she'd live in with him. Allie is already engaged to Lon and, in the two days she and Noah spend together, she must decide which man she wants.

The book focuses more heavily on the elderly couple, revealed to be Noah and Allie. Noah hopes that recounting their romance will rekindle her memory as she suffers from Alzheimer's. Leven expanded Allie's role in the movie and, aided by McAdams's performance, gave her more dimension compared to the book, where much of her story is recounted to Noah via letters and Noah's own memory of events. In the book, Allie gives a brief and to-the-point version of her final confrontation with Lon, but the film allows it to be seen.

Both the book and film present Lon as a man who certainly doesn't deserve to be hurt. The novel describes him as a kindhearted workaholic lawyer who meets Allie at a Christmas party and tells her he isn't looking for a serious relationship. He eventually changes his mind and wants to marry her. The movie further pumps him up as the perfect man, introducing him as a soldier wounded in the war who asks Allie out on a date while swathed in bandages. Lon tries to win Allie back in the book, but the reader is not privy to what that entails. In the movie, ever the gracious gentleman, Lon respects Allie's decision.

Allie's parents are seen as impediments stopping her relationship with Noah. The movie gives additional reasoning behind their interference. Allie's mother, Anne (Joan Allen), recounts to her daughter her own story of falling in love with a man of a lower class. She questions her own decisions in life before eventually giving Allie her blessing to be with Noah.

There are several comparisons between *The Notebook* and Robert James Waller's *The Bridges of Madison County*. Each is about a brief romance that takes place over a short period of time and has long-standing implications for the couple. But where Waller's book keeps his lovers apart, *The Notebook* goes in the opposite direction. Inspired by his wife's grandparents' sixty-year marriage, Sparks gives Noah and Allie a happy ending. Allie is considered medically unique with her severely degenerative condition—her doctors are surprised she remembers Noah at all, albeit in short spurts. In the book's final pages, Noah—after surviving a stroke—sneaks into Allie's room at night, hoping she won't be upset to see him. He goes to kiss her and Allie returns the kiss with the allusion that more intimacy will occur. Is it a miracle? Is Allie cured? Or is this another temporary respite? The book gives no definitive answer, but it's clear the couple are grateful for the time they have.

Cassavetes takes a more bittersweet route in the movie. Noah goes to Allie's room, where she recognizes him. The pair lie next to each other in bed and it's implied they've died together.

As both characters say throughout the book, they've never wanted anyone else, and each version of the story makes a fantastic argument about why Allie and Noah are perfect for each other. Sparks's novel may be different from Cassavates's beloved film, but they both tell the story of enduring love between a couple that has continued to charm audiences for decades.

BROKEBACK MOUNTAIN

2005

Directed by Ang Lee
Screenplay by Larry McMurtry and Diana Ossana
Based on "Brokeback Mountain" by Annie Proulx, 1997

"I wish I knew how to quit you."

Director Ang Lee's adaptation of Annie Proulx's story "Brokeback Mountain" has been praised for its groundbreaking exploration of homosexuality, opening the door for a wave of other mainstream LGBTQ+ features. The story follows the lives of two cowboys starting in 1963. Ennis del Mar (Heath Ledger) is a man of few words, while Jack Twist (Jake Gyllenhaal) is a loud, brash man prone to impulsive decisions. The two are sent up to herd and tend sheep on the eponymous mountain, where they fall into a romantic relationship that plays out over the course of several years. Regardless of their individual attempts to move on, the pull of Brokeback Mountain continues to draw them back to each other. Whether it be the film or the book, the story tells a tenderhearted story of how the heart wants what it wants, regardless of gender.

Proulx's story was published in the pages of *The New Yorker* in 1997. Like her other fiction stories, "Brokeback Mountain" uses its rural setting to show how individuals carve out their existence in a constantly changing world. Ennis and Jack have a love and respect for each other, but their individual lives (and the homophobia of the world in 1963) pull them apart. As Ennis himself says, "If you can't fix it, you've got to stand it." They try to live normal, heterosexual lives by getting married to women and having kids.

In just fifty-five pages, Proulx uses cultural details, geography, the landscape, history, and economy of the place to fill in all the necessary gaps a reader might have in order to emphasize that people can't be understood out of context. Every decision Jack and Ennis make in the story is fueled by their upbringing, their economic status, and their education, none of which are judged as good or bad. Their relationship being outside the mainstream of the period is also presented without judgment. Is it true love? Who knows. Either way, they have a connection to each other that cannot be erased.

Proulx's story starts in the moment, with Ennis del Mar preparing to move away. Much is inferred about who Ennis is. It's implied he's moved multiple times because of his inability to hold a steady job. He's resigned to living with his married daughter if he has to. This is the launchpad for the rest of the story, which plays out as Ennis recounts memories of his past with Jack. Since Ennis is the central protagonist, everything is filtered through his perspective. The reader learns exclusively about his life over the years—marrying his sweetheart Alma Beers (Michelle Williams), with whom he has two daughters—while Jack's history is told in snatches during the few times Ennis and Jack are together.

Everything contained in Proulx's narrative finds its way into the movie, but with a wider emphasis on each man's personal life in full, alongside their illicit romance because Proulx's story is so brief and limited in its perspective. Screenwriters Larry

McMurtry (author of *The Last Picture Show*) and Diana Ossana flesh out the narrative to show the viewer Ennis and Jack's stories in greater detail and balance them equally. Alongside Ennis's relationship with Alma, we see Jack's personal life as well. He spontaneously marries a woman named Lureen (Anne Hathaway), with whom he has a son, and struggles to assert himself against his domineering father-in-law.

Both versions examine how the characters grapple with their sexual identity, with Gyllenhaal himself saying in a 2006 interview with *Details* magazine that "I approached the story believing that these are actually two straight guys who fall in love." The movie shows Jack regularly going to Mexico to have sex with men, while in the book Jack refers to Mexico once during an argument with Ennis, believing they could have a more open relationship there.

The book sees Ennis and Jack routinely asserting their heterosexuality or questioning their sexuality. After their first encounter, Jack says that it was "a one-shot thing. Nobody's business but ours." Ennis later says that they must be straight because "I mean we both got wives and kids, right?" This is intentional on Proulx's part as her hope is that the reader looks at the story and uses it to reflect on their own personal attitudes, values, and hang-ups on the subject. The actors speaking these same lines on-screen do a bit more to emphasize that they are lying to each other and themselves.

Proulx writes the pair as having a lot in common.

Gyllenhaal said in an interview with *The Hollywood Reporter* that "what ties these two characters together is not just a love, but a loneliness." They're both "rough mannered and rough spoken" high school dropouts "with no prospects, brought up to hard work and privation." They also can't connect with their children. In the book, Jack discloses to Ennis that his son is dyslexic and Ennis—after Alma reveals that she always knew about his relationship with Jack—"didn't try to see his girls for a long time, figuring they would look him up when they got the sense and years to move out from Alma." Each man suffers from flaws that have nothing to do with their sexuality but are enhanced by the great lengths to which they go to keep it secret or avoid it.

Leonardo DiCaprio, Brad Pitt, and Ryan Phillippe were all considered for the lead roles at one point. Eventually, director Ang Lee came to the project and cast Ledger and Gyllenhaal, who, at twenty-six and twenty-five, respectively, were older than the characters in the novel, who meet before they each turn twenty. Interestingly, it is Gyllenhaal's Jack who is at odds, looks-wise, with his counterpart in Proulx's story. She describes Jack as having curly hair and buck teeth. Ennis doesn't have much physical description but is said to have a benign growth on his eye in his older years that causes his eyelid to droop, and a crooked nose due to a past break.

Both versions end with a similar sense of bittersweet tragedy. Jack dies after, according to Lureen, a car tire exploded in his face. Ennis wonders, though, if Jack was beaten to death with a tire iron by men who found out about his sexuality. Ennis wants to scatter Jack's ashes on Brokeback Mountain, but Jack's parents refuse to give Ennis the remains.

The movie ends with Ennis peering into his closet, where one of Jack's shirts now resides, tucked inside one of Ennis's, near a postcard of Brokeback Mountain. With tears in his eyes

Ennis simply says, "Jack, I swear..." Ennis is left to wonder what could have been as he holds on to an aching longing for a time and place that now lives only in his memory.

The novel adds a coda with Ennis having recurring dreams of Jack and his reminder that "If you can't fix it, you've got to stand it." In comparison to the movie, this coda punctuates the book's theme that relationships aren't static, and that the choices we make are the culmination of every moment and relationship we have (or don't have). Ennis is left to dream of Jack and wonder if both of them made the right choices, choices he can no longer change and must live with.

Brokeback Mountain won three Oscars out of eight nominations, for its screenplay, Ang Lee's direction, and its score. It lost Best Picture to *Crash* in one of the more controversial decisions in Oscars history. It opened the door to other movies that looked at LGBTQ+ issues, including *Capote* and *Breakfast on Pluto* in 2005 alone, and its impact continues to be felt in movies that tell queer stories today.

ATONEMENT

2007

Directed by Joe Wright
Screenplay by Christopher Hampton
Based on *Atonement* by Ian McEwan, 2001

"I love you. I'll wait for you. Come back. Come back to me."

Joe Wright's adaptation of Ian McEwan's romantic novel *Atonement* is a beautifully told story of dreams shattered in the wake of childhood ignorance. The story of thirteen-year-old Briony Tallis (Saorise Ronan) and her misinterpretation of an incident between her older sister Cecilia (Keira Knightly) and Robbie (James McAvoy), the son of their housekeeper, one night in 1935 is a sweeping, romantic meditation on the nature of forgiveness. Briony, as an adult, spends the novel trying to—as the title implies—atone for what she's done, but reconciles with the fact that she forever changed the lives of two people she loved dearly.

Director Joe Wright had a tall order to fill when he decided to tackle McEwan's text, considering the multilayered themes at its center, but from Seamus McGarvey's Oscar-nominated cinematography to Kiera Knightley's performance (and the iconic green dress she wears designed by Jacqueline Durran), he more than succeeded. Screenwriter Christopher Hampton's first stab at adapting McEwan's book was a more "conventional [and] literary approach," the screenwriter said in a 2007 interview. It had a linear structure, with a grown Briony providing voiceover and an epilogue featuring an elderly Briony woven throughout the film.

When Wright came aboard, he wanted to move away from contemporary filmmaking to create something more historical and akin to McEwan's fragmented text. Hampton's second run at the screenplay hewed closer to the novel and, as seen in the movie, presents Briony's version of events before flashing back to what actually took place between Cecilia and Robbie. Briony watches from an upstairs window as Cecilia strips to her underwear and jumps into a fountain. Unable to hear what they're saying, Briony believes Robbie has forced Cecilia to do it, instead of what truly happened, shown in a later scene wherein Cecilia jumps into the fountain to collect a broken vase fragment out of pride. This confused moment comes to a head during the book and movie's central conflict, when Briony walks in on what she believes is Robbie raping her sister. The actual scene, the pair making love, is then shown.

After Robbie is arrested for then allegedly raping Briony's cousin Lola (Juno Temple), as accused by Briony, the second half of the book and movie look into Robbie's time at Dunkirk, his eventual reunion with Cecilia, and a now eighteen-year-old Briony (Romola Garai) working as a nurse, estranged from her sister because of her accusation against Robbie.

The movie is ambiguous regarding how much of Briony's actions are the result of childhood ignorance and how much is jealousy because Robbie fancies Cecilia and not her. The book doesn't quibble that Briony chose to accuse Robbie of rape out of a desire to be the central character in her own story. In the book, she says that while she didn't see Robbie with her own eyes, the way she came to accuse him—reading a vulgar letter he mistakenly gave to her for Cecilia—is too complex to tell the police. Briony says it's easier to stick to saying she actually saw him.

McEwan's novel is a dense exploration of perception versus reality, as well as how storytellers blend fact and fiction, not unlike filmmaking itself. For Briony, storytelling is a form of control and she treats everyone in her life as if they are characters in a book she's writing. If they don't conform to her preconceived plots, she can't make sense of anything. Briony is more worried that Robbie will be labeled a hero for finding her cousins—who ran away from home during that same fateful night—and diminish her accusations.

Because the cinematic medium doesn't allow for divergences that aren't necessary to the plot, many of the storytelling cues Briony peppers throughout the book that indicate the story might be fictional are left on the cutting room floor, specifically the way Briony plays with the Tallis family history and inner monologue. The absent Tallis matriarch, Emily (Harriet Walter), who only has a few stray scenes in the movie, gets added introspection in the book. Emily worries about her children—why her son has taken a civil service job, that Cecilia won't marry because she's too introverted and smokes, and Briony having an inability to handle failure. It's never clear whether any of this is true to her character, or Briony thinking like her mother.

These moments, perceived as part of a book with a third-person narrator, are eventually revealed to be inventions of Briony's mind, making the reader question how much she is inventing for entertainment value. Briony makes up what her mother and others are thinking, continuing to control a story she says she wants to tell honestly. When Robbie and Cecilia fight over the vase in front of the fountain, the book pivots to a story about how the vase was given to their uncle Clem during

World War I by grateful villagers and how it made its way to the family for safekeeping.

When the audience realizes that the story they're being told is the plot of an elderly Briony's (Vanessa Redgrave) final book, it hits like a ton of bricks. That impact isn't dulled in the book as the reader sees, at the end of part 3, the initials "B. T." and the year "1999." These thoughts are what Briony was thinking at the time, written by a woman who is now older and wiser. The ending of the book shows Briony's attempt to find forgiveness in herself now that Cecilia and Robbie are dead, and give them a happy ending they were denied in life.

The epilogue is extended in McEwan's novel. The reader learns that Briony's cousin Lola, now grown, is married to Paul (Benedict Cumberbatch), the man who actually assaulted her the night Briony accused Robbie. It is Lola's assault that justified Briony in her belief that Robbie is a rapist. Paul and Lola, now Lord and Lady Marshall, are extremely wealthy and philanthropic, but highly litigious. The movie's end sees Briony promoting her final book and planning to retire, as she is dying of vascular dementia. McEwan's novel further adds that to avoid a lawsuit, Briony is unable to publish her book at all until the Marshalls are dead. Since Briony herself is dying, this means the book will be released after her death as well.

Briony sees memory as fractured and fleeting in the book. People choose to remember what they want to remember. Eventually, as age and death come closer, everyone—the Marshalls, Briony, Robbie, and Cecilia—will soon only be an invention of someone's memory. Briony gives Robbie and Cecilia a happy ending that tries to make up for both dying young and tragically—him at Dunkirk and her drowning during the bombing and flooding of a London subway station—as a result of Briony's false allegations. Who knows if either of them would have been in those situations otherwise. As elderly Briony says in the film, "What sense of hope or satisfaction could a reader derive . . . I gave them their happiness." The film's final image is of Robbie and Cecilia, forever ensconced in their own private world, relaxing on a beach. The book ends as Briony celebrates her seventy-seventh birthday and pictures Cecilia and Robbie, in love, at her party. For Briony, the pair live on forever with her.

TWILIGHT

2008

Directed by Catherine Hardwicke
Screenplay by Melissa Rosenberg
Based on *Twilight* by Stephenie Meyer, 2005

"And so the lion fell in love with the lamb."

Vampires have straddled the line between horror and romance since their earliest inceptions in film, from Bram Stoker's *Dracula* to Anne Rice's *Interview with the Vampire*. The fanged fiends who lust for blood have represented sexual desire or passion, a loss of innocence, and forbidden fruit for the characters stuck in their thrall. Stephenie Meyer's 2005 novel *Twilight* took these familiar themes and applied them to a Romeo and Juliet–esque love story that became a global phenomenon.

The story of mortal girl Bella Swan (Kristen Stewart) and the vampire Edward Cullen (Robert Pattinson) takes Shakespeare's story and uses it to look at who we choose to love and the lengths we'll go to be with that person. Bella Swan has recently moved to Forks, Washington. She soon meets Edward Cullen, a social outcast alongside his four siblings. Bella learns that Edward is a vampire and wants to be with him, but he is convinced they can't be together despite her protests to the contrary. As Edward tries to contain his lust for Bella's blood, he also must protect her from other vampires who wish to do her harm.

Author Stephenie Meyer said the idea for *Twilight* came to her in a dream in 2003. What started out as a single chapter turned into a five-hundred-page book within three months.

Meyer was a fan of classic literature, naming the vampire Edward after both Edward Rochester from Charlotte Brontë's *Jane Eyre*, and Edward Ferrars from Jane Austen's *Sense and Sensibility*. The novel, published in 2005, became a *New York Times* bestseller within a month. The manuscript, at the time unpublished, had made its way to MTV Films the previous year, where Mark Lord was tasked with writing a screenplay. He crafted a version that had little in common with Meyer's novel, turning Bella into a long-distance runner and having her seek revenge against the vampires that killed her father. She is turned into a vampire herself and rides "jet skis while being chased by the FBI." In a 2022 interview, Lord said the studio "wanted to just put in some more action to advance it more and give something more for the male audience. They thought they were going to lose the male audience with too much of a romance."

The adaptation went nowhere until Summit Entertainment purchased the rights in 2007. Director Catherine Hardwicke was brought on to the project, as well as screenwriter Melissa Rosenberg, with a caveat stipulated by Meyer that no vampire fangs could be shown and no one dies in the film who isn't killed in the original book. Rosenberg knew adapting the book required some skill. It didn't just have to lure in new audiences, it also had to be faithful enough not to turn off the readers who had already fallen in love with Bella and Edward. "Our intent all along was to stay true to the book," she said in a 2008 interview. "And it has less to do with adapting it word for word and more with making sure the characters' arcs and emotional journeys are the same."

Many of the changes involved condensing several of Bella's friends into single characters for the movie. Jessica, played memorably by Anna Kendrick, is a combination of Bella's friends Jessica and Lauren. And while most fans are aware of the love triangle between Bella (Kristen Stewart), Edward (Robert Pattinson), and Jacob Black (Taylor Lautner), the book has another romance plot involving Forks high schoolers Eric, Mike, and Tyler, who all vie for Bella's attention as well. Rosenberg also had to make static scenes more energetic for a movie. Bella discovers Edward is a vampire while they're sitting in a car—not the most interesting of locations. Rosenberg moved the discussion to an open field, where Edward could show off why he doesn't go to school on sunny days: because his skin sparkles like a diamond.

The book spends much time exploring Edward and Bella's relationship, specifically Edward's internal push and pull between his love for Bella and his vampiric need to consume her blood. But conventional villains arrive in the form of vampires James (Cam Gigandet) and Victoria (Rachelle Lefevre), the complete opposites of the vegetarian Cullen clan. The novel has them arrive in chapter 18, six chapters before the end. Such a delayed introduction doesn't work in a movie, so the pair is shown earlier killing a Forks resident, which immediately sets them up as the primary antagonists.

The Cullens themselves also have an extensive backstory exclusive to Meyer's novel that establishes the rules of the vampire family. As Edward explains to Bella, his makeshift father

Carlisle (Peter Facinelli) only turns those who are dying into vampires. Edward was turned during the 1918 Spanish flu epidemic, a moment recounted on-screen. The reader also learns that Carlisle's wife Esme (Elizabeth Reaser) jumped off a cliff after her baby died before Carlisle saved her, and Edward's "brother" Emmett (Kellan Lutz) was turned by fellow Cullen Alice (Ashley Greene), after he was attacked by a bear.

Alice also has a separate subplot in the novel. Though she has the ability to see the future, Alice doesn't recall her life before meeting the Cullens and becoming a vampire. James later tells Bella in the third act that he tried to hunt Alice, who was living in an asylum. Carlisle turned Alice into a vampire in order to keep James from killing her.

The love triangle between Bella, Edward, and Jacob highlights Bella's struggle between two different paths—immortality and passion with Edward, or humanity and stability with Jacob. This triangle is explored in greater psychological depth in the book, with Bella's internal monologues offering insight into her conflicting emotions and the weight of her choices. The film visually emphasizes the tension and romantic rivalry but streamlines much of Bella's introspection in favor of dramatic moments. As a result, the movie presents the triangle in a more action-driven way, while the book delves deeper into Bella's emotional and moral dilemmas.

The novel ends with Bella disappointed to go to prom with Edward, more interested in wanting to be a vampire. Alice had a prophecy that Edward would turn Bella, and the teenager hoped he would do it before the big dance. A franchise from the onset, the end also sets up a sequel with Victoria planning to avenge James's death after the Cullens killed him in defense of Bella. The old-fashioned romance told for a millennial audience played on familiar themes of forbidden romance that seemed fresh thanks to a slick cinematic style.

Meyer's final three novels in the series were also adapted: *New Moon* in 2009, *Eclipse* in 2010, and *Breaking Dawn*, split into two parts, in 2011 and 2012. Meyer retold the same story from Edward's point of view in the 2020 novel *Midnight Sun*, which has yet to be adapted, and she's even written a gender-swapped version (with a female vampire and a male human), *Life and Death: Twilight Reimagined*, published in 2015.

The film's success, and the phenomenon that it became thanks to the movie's marketing and lead actors, not only sparked a frenzy of young-adult film adaptations but compelled authors to write books inspired by *Twilight* itself. In 2011, *Fifty Shades of Grey* hit bookshelves. The erotic romance was initially written online by author E. L. James as *Twilight* fan fiction before becoming an actual book. That series would be adapted into a three-film franchise starting in 2015.

CAROL

2015

Directed by Todd Haynes
Screenplay by Phyllis Nagy
Based on *The Price of Salt* by
Patricia Highsmith, 1952

"My angel. Flung out of space."

Author Patricia Highsmith is best known for noirish thrillers like *The Talented Mr. Ripley* and *Strangers on a Train*. So when she wrote *The Price of Salt* in 1951, her agent saw it as career suicide. The author of *Strangers on a Train*, a film that already had a queer subtext running through it, wanted to publish a story about a lesbian romance? It was a stretch, to say the least. So much so that when the book was eventually published in 1952, it was under the pen name of Claire Morgan to protect Highsmith's literary reputation and avoid the criminality of homosexuality at the time. (It wasn't until 1983 that the novel, rereleased under Highsmith's preferred title, *Carol*, was published under her actual name.)

The Price of Salt tells the story of shopgirl Therese Belivet (Rooney Mara), who falls for cool housewife Carol Aird (Cate Blanchett). Carol is going through a contentious divorce and trying to hold on to custody of her daughter. But as the two's relationship develops it threatens to change their lives, for good and ill.

Highsmith based *The Price of Salt* on a 1948 encounter she had with Kathleen Wiggins Senn while working in the toy department of Bloomingdale's. Highsmith also drew from other past relationships, like that of Philadelphia socialite Virginia Kent Catherwood, who eventually lost custody of her own daughter, and psychoanalyst Kathryn Hamill Cohen. In a way, the book is somewhat autobiographical, though it holds much in common with Highsmith's previous suspense novels in how it follows aloof characters harboring dark secrets no one else can know about, and the lies told to keep them.

It took over sixty years for an adaptation of Highsmith's novel to hit the big screen due to its subject matter. Theatre de Lys manager Terese Hayden attempted to make the movie in the 1950s. She wrote a treatment, tentatively titled *Winter Journey*, with the story changing to a heterosexual romance following a man named Carl. The attempt was "apparently unsuccessful," according to Hayden, and didn't go anywhere. Decades later screenwriter Phyllis Nagy, a friend of Highsmith's, took to writing an adaptation. "What still strikes me now is how radical it was in terms of its overall conception," Nagy said in a 2015 interview. "Two central figures not giving a rat's ass about sexual identity. No one frets about being gay; others fret on their behalf." Nagy refused to make the characters feel guilty about being gay, refused to include any breakdown-type scenes, and wanted the happy ending from the book retained.

Much like Highsmith's other books, secrecy and suspicion run parallel to Therese and Carol's relationship. When Therese first meets Carol, she is desperate to keep her a secret, even from Therese's boyfriend, Richard. "She didn't want Richard to know about Carol, or even ever meet her." This desire is due to Therese's all-consuming love and obsession for Carol, as well as the fear of having their relationship discovered. When Richard learns about the couple, he considers the relationship unnatural, as does Carol's husband, Harge (Kyle Chandler).

For Highsmith, their relationship is dangerous because it's perceived societally as abnormal and inappropriate. (The United States would start decriminalizing homosexuality on a state-by-state basis starting in 1962.) In a bid to be alone, Carol and Therese take a road trip across the country, constantly dodging a detective sent on behalf of Harge to spy on and record them in preparation for Carol's custody case. Carol and Therese are forced to reserve their love for each other for private spaces, like houses and hotel rooms, or among like-minded people like Carol's former lover, Abby (Sarah Paulson).

Abby in the book is Carol's closest confidante, but their romantic relationship is brief, limited to just a few months, as opposed to the allusions in the film that they have been together for years. Harge is also humanized further in the movie, where he's a sympathetic if misguided and hurt man, who does love his wife. In the book, Harge is seen only through Therese's eyes and thus comes off as a cold and cruel villain.

Because of more modern conceptions of queer characters as three-dimensional people, Nagy's version of *Carol* isn't a story of obsession or unrequited love. Both the book and the film are straightforward love stories about two people who love each other, regardless of what society says or how it tries to force them apart. This message comes through with the way Nagy moved the timeline further into 1952–1953, making stronger connections to the Eisenhower era and the communist blacklist. For Nagy, this era was fraught with paranoia and pressure to conform. Carol and Therese are similar to those called in front of the House Un-American Activities Committee who refused to name names (i.e., out anyone).

Therese's life is described as "a series of zigzags" and, as her relationship with Carol develops, everyone—Carol included—mentions how much Therese needs to grow up. When Carol tells

Therese she agreed to give up her relationship with the younger woman in order to keep her child, Therese becomes upset. She believes Carol has "chosen" her daughter over her and ignores Carol's own words that having a husband and child means having to make uncomfortable decisions. Therese decides to spend time on her own in South Dakota, not immediately returning to New York as she does in the movie. She gets her own job, changes her appearance, and starts living for herself, not Carol. When the two eventually reunite in New York, Carol explains that she and Harge have worked out custody of their daughter and, with that solved, she asks Therese to live with her. Therese refuses and start to rebuild her life in New York.

Carol and Therese's reunion in both versions is a happy ending in that two people, whom others tried so hard to keep apart, find their way back to each other. The film sees the two go to dinner, but they get interrupted by a friend of Therese's. Still resistant to truly embrace Carol and resume a relationship, Therese leaves to go to a party with friends, but she fails to connect with anyone there. The only one she wants is Carol, causing her to return to the restaurant where Carol waits for her. The book is similar, albeit Therese flirts with an English actress at the party only to realize she doesn't have the same feelings for this woman as she does for Carol. She rushes back to meet Carol, who is waiting for her with a smile on her face. The book ends with Therese finally willing to not only reciprocate Carol's love, but accept herself.

Carol and *The Price of Salt* remain groundbreaking examples of their respective eras. Each reiterates the principle that "love is love," but because of the mores of the 1950s Highsmith is cooler about the relationship, more introspective. She also makes her story one of maturation and self-acceptance. The film takes those same themes and gives viewers a more modern conception, one that shows that, in the end, love wins every time.

Acknowledgments

When I wrote the first volume of *But Have You Read the Book?* I had dreamed I'd write a follow-up but never anticipated it would happen so soon! I wrote the first book in less than six months with the "benefit" of a pandemic, a feat I didn't think I could (or would want to) do again. But reading these forty books, with a little more time than the first go-round, has made me realize what I'm capable of as a writer. My college studying skills still have some use!

I have to thank Cindy Sipala and Randall Lotowycz for wanting me to come back for Volume 2! The entire Running Press team has spoiled me with encouragement, feedback, and support going back to the first *But Have You Read.*

I also have to shout out TCM. You are more than a network to me. The company has given me so many firsts, whether that's my first interview, my first film festival trip, or the first time I was ever on the air, that I can never thank them enough for. The fact that I got to write my first book for them was a full-circle moment and I'm honored every day to be a part of the "TCM library." Also, I appreciate you for psychically knowing when I needed a reading break and airing a John Garfield movie when I needed it.

Mom. I know I'm legally required to thank you for everything, starting with my birth, but I hope you realize how much I appreciate and love you. You talked me off the ledge of how I'd get this book done so many times. Thank you for always knowing when I'd need a snack, a walk, or a break. And throwing in a thanks for my brothers, John and Steven. You guys didn't do anything in regards to this book but . . . here ya are.

Thank you to my agent, Mark Falkin. You took a chance on me back in 2023 and we've been on a roll ever since. Thank you for advocating for me when I needed it and helping me navigate how to squeeze this into a packed schedule.

My fantastic friends, Tony and Emily. You guys have kept me sane over the last two years as I've been writing several books. Thanks for always lending an ear. Emily, thank you for indulging my chronic texts asking for advice. You've helped me more than you know.

Bibliography

Arau, Alfonso, dir. *Like Water for Chocolate*. Miramax, 1992.

Arnold, Jeremy. "Tess on Blu-Ray." Turner Classic Movies, 25 Sept. 2014. www.tcm.com/tcmdb/title/92614/tess#articles-reviews?articleId=1036097.

Austen, Jane. *Pride and Prejudice*. Salem Press, 1813.

The Author Speaks: Selected PW Interviews, 1967–1976. Bowker, 1978.

Axmaker, Sean. "The Ghost and Mrs. Muir." Turner Classic Movies, November 8, 2013. www.tcm.com/tcmdb/title/76188/the-ghost-and-mrs-muir#articles-reviews?articleId=906598.

Axmaker, Sean. "Pierrot Le Fou—Jean-Luc Godard's 1965 Masterpiece on DVD." Turner Classic Movies, November 19, 2007. www.tcm.com/tcmdb/title/86685/pierrot-le-fou#articles-reviews?articleId=187441.

Behlmer, Rudy. *Memo from David O. Selznick*. Viking Press, 1972.

Blixen, Karen. *Out of Africa*. Stellar Books/Stellar Classics, 2018.

"Boris Pasternak—Facts." Nobel Prize Outreach 2025. NobelPrize.org, February 5, 2025. www.nobelprize.org/prizes/literature/1958/pasternak/facts/.

Bosman, Julie. "To Use and Use Not." *New York Times*, 4 July 2012. www.nytimes.com/2012/07/05/books/a-farewell-to-arms-with-hemingways-alternate-endings.html.

Brody, Richard. "Pierrot Le Fou: Self-Portrait in a Shattered Lens." The Criterion Collection, September 22, 2009. www.criterion.com/current/posts/525-pierrot-le-fou-self-portrait-in-a-shattered-lens.

Brontë, Charlotte. *Jane Eyre*. Pearson Education, 2008.

Brown, Clarence, dir. *Anna Karenina*. Metro-Goldwyn-Mayer, 1935.

Brown, Emma, and John Calendo. "New Again: Kim Novak." *Interview Magazine*, February 15, 2012. www.interviewmagazine.com/film/new-again-kim-novak.

Bubbeo, Daniel. *The Women of Warner Brothers*. McFarland, 2010.

Canby, Vincent. "Screen Perfection and a 'Love Story': Erich Segal's Romantic Tale Begins Run." *New York Times*, December 18, 1970. www.nytimes.com/1970/12/18/archives/screen-perfection-and-a-love-storyerich-segals-romantic-tale-begins.html.

Canfield, David. "'Atonement': The Inside Story on That Iconic Green Dress." *Entertainment Weekly*, July 5, 2022. www.ew.com/movies/2017/12/07/atonement-10th-anniversary-green-dress/.

Capote, Truman. *Breakfast at Tiffany's*. Vintage, 2012.

Carroll, Larry. "'Twilight' Author Stephenie Meyer Recalls Robert Pattinson Spat, Seeing Movie the First Time." MTV, November 14, 2008. www.mtv.com/movies/news/articles/1599282/20081113/story.jhtml.

Carroll, Larry. "'Twilight' Tuesday: Screenwriter Melissa Rosenberg Was Inspired by 'Brokeback Mountain.'" MTV, September 16, 2008.

Caspary, Vera. *Laura*. 1943. Feminist Press at CUNY, 2005.

Cassavetes, Nick, dir. *The Notebook*. New Line Cinema, 2004.

Churchwell, Sarah. "Breakfast at Tiffany's: When Audrey Hepburn Won Marilyn Monroe's Role." *The Guardian*, September 4, 2009. www.theguardian.com/books/2009/sep/05/breakfast-at-tiffanys-audrey-hepburn.

Clark, Anne Victoria. "Brad Pitt, Leonardo DiCaprio, Matt Damon, and Ryan Phillipe Turned Down *Brokeback Mountain*." *Vulture*, July 19, 2018. www.vulture.com/2018/07/here-are-the-a-listers-who-turned-down-brokeback-mountain.html.

Clarke, Gerald. *Capote: A Biography*. Carroll & Graf, 2005.

Complex, Valerie. "'How Stella Got Her Groove Back' at 25: Angela Bassett & Kevin Sullivan on Taye Diggs' Casting, Whoopi Goldberg's Generosity & Film's Lasting Impact—Tribeca." *Deadline*, June 18, 2023. www.deadline.com/2023/06/tribeca-festival-storytellers-angela-bassett-how-stella-got-her-groove-back-1235419805/.

Crowther, Bosley. "Adaptation of Pasternak Novel at the Capitol." *New York Times*, December 23, 1965. www.nytimes.com/1965/12/23/archives/adaptation-of-pasternak-novel-at-the-capitol-by-bosley-crowther.html.

Cukor, George, dir. *Camille*. MGM, 1936.

Custodio, Isabel. "How Breakfast at Tiffany's Turned into a Totally Different Movie: Adapting a Classic." *YouTube*, August 31, 2021. www.youtube.com/watch?v=0Gs-l6yHKHY.

Dans, Peter E. *Christians in the Movies: A Century of Saints and Sinners*. Rowman & Littlefield, 2009.

Dawson, Jill. "Carol: The Women Behind Patricia Highsmith's Lesbian Novel." *The Guardian*, May 13, 2015. www.theguardian.com/books/2015/may/13/patricia-highsmith-film-adaptation-carol-only-openly-lesbian-novel-cannes-cate-blanchett.

Diaz de Chumaceiro, Cora L. "Maude Adam's Portrait as Muse for Richard Matheson." *Creativity Research Journal* 17, no. 2/3 (2005): 297–8.

Dick, R. A. *The Ghost and Mrs. Muir.* Vintage, 2014.

Didžiulytė, Margarita. *Imitation and Parody of the Victorian Novel in John Fowles's "The French Lieutenant's Woman."* Vilnius University Master Paper, 2006.

Doll, Susan. "The French Lieutenant's Woman." Turner Classic Movies, May 4, 2009. www.tcm.com/tcmdb/title/16932/the-french-lieutenants-woman#articles-reviews?articleId=240887.

Dreiser, Theodore. *An American Tragedy.* E-BOOKARAMA, 2019.

du Maurier, Daphne. *My Cousin Rachel.* Kindle Unlimited, 2025.

Dumas, Alexandre. *Camille: The Lady of the Camellias.* Books on Demand, 2020.

Eastwood, Clint, dir. *The Bridges of Madison County.* Warner Bros., 1995.

The Eddie Mannix Ledger. Los Angeles: Margaret Herrick Library, Center for Motion Picture Study.

Edwards, Blake, dir. *Breakfast at Tiffany's.* Paramount Pictures, 1961.

Eliot, Marc. *American Rebel: The Life of Clint Eastwood.* Random House, 2010.

Emery, Robert J. *The Directors: In Their Own Words.* TV Books, 1999.

Emrys, A. B. "All My Lives: Vera Caspary's Life, Times and Fiction." Afterword to *Laura*, by Vera Caspary. Feminist Press at CUNY, 2005.

Erickson, Glenn. "Joan Fontaine in the 1944 Film Version of Jane Eyre." Turner Classic Movies, May 1, 2007. www.tcm.com/tcmdb/title/79673/jane-eyre#articles-reviews?articleId=172099.

Esquivel, Laura. *Like Water for Chocolate.* Black Swan, 1989.

Fielding, Helen. *Bridget Jones's Diary.* Penguin, 1996.

Fields, Jack. "Jane Seymour on 'Somewhere in Time.'" FieldsonFilm, April 23, 2022. www.youtube.com/watch?v=MVrOUk8Mt5Y.

Fitzpatrick, Sheila. "The Zhivago Affair: The Kremlin, the CIA, and the Battle over a Forbidden Book." *The Guardian*, June 18, 2014. www.theguardian.com/books/2014/jun/18/zhivago-affair-kremlin-cia-battle-forbidden-book-peter-finn-petra-couvee-review.

Fleming, Michael. "'Zorro' Marks Sequel." *Variety*, March 23, 2001. www.variety.com/2001/film/features/zorro-marks-sequel-1117795799/.

Fleming, Victor, dir. *Gone with the Wind.* Metro-Goldwyn-Mayer, 1939.

Focus News. "Production Notes—*Atonement*." *Focus Features*, January 19, 2010. www.focusfeatures.com/article/production_notes___atonement.

Foerster, Jonathan. "Shirley MacLaine Isn't Getting Old, She's Just Advanced." *Naples News*, February 9, 2011.

Forster, E. M. *Maurice*. Hodder & Stoughton, 2011.

Forster, E. M. *A Room with a View*. Penguin Classics, 2000.

Fowles, John. "The French Lieutenant's Diary." *Granta* 86: Film, 2004.

Fowles, John. *The French Lieutenant's Woman*. Little, Brown, 2012.

Friedrich, Otto. *City of Nets: Portrait of Hollywood in the 1940s*. University of California Press, 1986.

Fristoe, Roger. "A Farewell to Arms (1957)." Turner Classic Movies, October 16, 2013. www.tcm.com/tcmdb /title/74575/a-farewell-to-arms#articles-reviews?articleId=719922.

Fristoe, Roger. "Gone with the Wind." Turner Classic Movies, June 25, 2003. www.tcm.com/tcmdb/title/414427 /gone-with-the-wind#articles-reviews?articleId=535.

Fristoe, Roger. "Love Story" Turner Classic Movies, January 24, 2006. www.tcm .com/tcmdb/title/4689/love story#articles-reviews?articleId=88484.

Galloway, Stephen. "10 Years After 'Brokeback,' Jake Gyllenhaal Remembers Heath Ledger: 'Way Beyond His Years as a Human.'" *Hollywood Reporter*, November 25, 2015. www.hollywoodreporter.com/movies/movie-news /ten-years-brokeback-jake-gyllenhaal-843951/.

Godard, Jean-Luc, dir. *Pierrot Le Fou*. Pathe Contemporary Films, 1965.

Grant, Lee. "Ryan O'Neal: A Love-Hate Story." *Los Angeles Times*, August 28, 1977.

Grossman, Lev. "Stephenie Meyer: A New J. K. Rowling?" *Time*, April 24, 2008. www.time.com/archive/6684537/stephenie-meyer-a-new-j-k-rowling/.

Hallström, Lasse, dir. *Chocolat*. Miramax, 2000.

Hampton, Christopher. "Atonement, So Good I Adapted It Twice." *The Guardian*, August 10, 2007. www.theguardian.com/film/filmblog/2007 /aug/10/atonementsogoodiadaptedittwice.

Hardy, Thomas. *Tess of the d'Urbervilles*. Createspace Independent Publishers, n.d. Originally published in 1891.

Hardwicke, Catherine, dir. *Twilight*. Summit Entertainment, 2008.

Harris, Joanne. *Chocolat: A Novel*. Penguin, 1999.

Hart, Hugh. "A Part with Meat on Its Bones." *Los Angeles Times*, April 8, 2001. web.archive.org/web/20131230232821/articles.latimes.com/2001/apr/08/entertainment/ca-48232/2.

Haynes, Todd, dir. *Carol*. Weinstein Company, 2015.

Heiman, Sarah. "Out of Africa." Turner Classic Movies, October 24, 2002. www.tcm.com/tcmdb/title/19122/out-of-africa#articles-reviews?articleId=1138.

Hemingway, Ernest. *A Farewell to Arms*. Scribner, 1929.

Highfill, Samantha. "Yes, George Clooney Almost Played Ryan Gosling's Noah in *The Notebook*." *Entertainment Weekly*, October 18, 2020. www.ew.com/movies/george-clooney-the-notebook-noah/.

Highsmith, Patricia. *The Price of Salt*. Dover, 2015.

Hiller, Arthur, dir. *Love Story*. Paramount Pictures, 1970.

Hilton, James. *Random Harvest*. Sanage, 2020.

Hirsch, Foster. *Otto Preminger: The Man Who Would Be King*. Screen Classics, 2021.

Hoffman, Barbara. "50 Years Later, 'The Graduate' Cast Reveals Behind-the-Scenes Secrets." *New York Post*, April 20, 2017. www.nypost.com/2017/04/20/50-years-later-the-graduate-cast-reveals-behind-the-scenes-secrets/.

Hull, E. M. *The Sheik*. Pine Street Books, 2001.

Ingersoll, Earl G. *Filming Forster: The Challenges of Adapting E. M. Forster's Novels for the Screen*. Rowman & Littlefield, 2012.

Ivory, James, dir. *Maurice*. Cinecom Pictures, 1987.

Ivory, James, dir. *A Room with a View*. Cinecom Pictures, 1985.

Jones, Belinda. "Rockumentaries . . ." *Empire*, January 1999.

Jordan, Louis. "*Carol*'s Happy Ending." *Slate*, November 19, 2015. www.slate.com/culture/2015/11/carol-screenwriter-phyllis-nagy-friend-of-patricia-highsmith-worked-for-20-years-to-get-the-film-made.html.

Kellaway, Kate. "Daphne's Unruly Passions." *The Guardian*, April 14, 2007. www.theguardian.com/books/2007/apr/15/fiction.features1.

Klady, Leonard. "Cinefile; 'Chocolat' Meanders Toward B.O. Record." *Variety*, April 12, 1994.

Koster, Henry, dir. *The Bishop's Wife*. Samuel Goldwyn Productions, 1947.

Koster, Henry, dir. *My Cousin Rachel*. Twentieth Century Fox, 1952.

Laman, Lisa. "Why Is *The Notebook*'s Ending Different on Streaming?" *Collider*, May 16, 2022. www.collider.com/the-notebook-movie-ending-different-explained/.

Lambert, Gavin. "The Making of Gone with the Wind (Part I)." *The Atlantic*, February 1973. www.theatlantic.com/magazine/archive/1973/02/the-making-of-gone-with-the-wind-part-i/306455/.

Landazuri, Margarita. "A Room with a View." Turner Classic Movies, November 10, 2009. www.tcm.com/tcmdb/title/88627/a-room-with-a-view#articles-reviews?articleId=276931.

Landazuri, Margarita. "Tess." Turner Classic Movies, November 8, 2013. www.tcm.com/tcmdb/title/92614/tess#articles-reviews?articleId=906558.

Landazuri, Margarita. "Women in Love." Turner Classic Movies, January 9, 2014. www.tcm.com/tcmdb/title/16931/women-in-love#articles-reviews?articleId=941265.

Lawrence, D. H. *Women in Love*. Penguin Classics, 1990.

Lean, David, dir. *Doctor Zhivago*. Warner Bros., 1965.

Lee, Ang, dir. *Brokeback Mountain*. Focus Features, 2005.

Leonard, Elmore. *Out of Sight*. Delacorte Press, 1996.

LeRoy, Mervyn, dir. *Random Harvest*. MGM, 1942.

Levy, Emanuel. *George Cukor: Master of Elegance: Hollywood's Legendary Director and His Stars*. William Morrow, 1994.

Leaming, Barbara. *Orson Welles: A Biography*. New York: Limelight, 1995.

Leonard, Robert Z., dir. *Pride and Prejudice*. Metro-Goldwyn-Mayer, 1940.

Lintz, Bernadette C. "Concocting La Dame aux camelias: Blood, Tears, and Other Fluids." *Nineteenth Century French Studies* 33, no. 3 (Spring–Summer 2005): 287–307. doi.org/10.1353/ncf.2005.0022. Accessed April 29, 2022.

LoBianco, Lorraine. "Bridget Jones's Diary (2001)." Turner Classic Movies, December 9, 2021. www.tcm.com/tcmdb/title/451029/bridget-joness-diary#articles-reviews?articleId=021531.

LoBianco, Lorraine. "The English Patient." Turner Classic Movies, July 7, 2014. www.tcm.com/tcmdb/title/300914/the-english-patient#articles-reviews?articleId=1014808.

Long, Robert Emmett. *The Films of Merchant Ivory*. Abrams, 1991.

Long, Robert Emmett. *James Ivory in Conversation: How Merchant Ivory Makes Its Movies*. University of California Press, 2005.

Looser, Devoney. *The Making of Jane Austen*. Johns Hopkins University Press, 2017.

"'Love Story' Didn't Start Out as a Book." *Star-Gazette*, December 19, 1970.

Maguire, Sharon, dir. *Bridget Jones's Diary*. Miramax, 2001.

Mankiewicz, Joseph L., dir. *Dragonwyck*. Twentieth Century Fox, 1946.

Mankiewicz, Joseph L., dir. *The Ghost and Mrs. Muir*. Twentieth Century Fox, 1947.

Martin, Pete. "How Grant Took Hollywood." *The Saturday Evening Post*, February 19, 1949. www.carygrant.net/articles/tookhollywood.htm.

Matheson, Richard. *Bid Time Return*. Tom Doherty Associates, 2008.

Maxford, Howard. *David Lean*. Batsford Books, 2000.

McEwan, Ian. *Atonement*. Anchor, 2003.

McHenry, Jackson. "Like Water for Chocolate Book Sequels and Musical Are Getting Cooked." *Vulture*, October 7, 2020. www.vulture.com/2020/10/like-water-for-chocolate-book-sequels-musical.html.

McMillan, Terry. *How Stella Got Her Groove Back*. Berkley, 2004.

McMillan, Terry. *Waiting to Exhale*. New American Library, 2011.

Melford, George, dir. *The Sheik*. Paramount Pictures, 1921.

Meyer, Stephenie. *Twilight*. Little, Brown Books for Young Readers, 2007.

Miller, Frank. "The Big Idea—Doctor Zhivago (1965)." Turner Classic Movies, July 26, 2004. www.tcm.com/tcmdb/title/129/doctor-zhivago#articles-reviews?articleId=71628.

Miller, Frank. "The Big Idea—Random Harvest." Turner Classic Movies, May 18, 2004. www.tcm.com/tcmdb/title/2716/random-harvest#articles-reviews?articleId=71665.

Miller, Frank. "Carol (2015)." Turner Classic Movies, March 29, 2021. www.tcm.com/tcmdb/title/980170/carol#articles-reviews?articleId=021188.

Miller, Frank. "The Essentials—Doctor Zhivago (1965)." Turner Classic Movies, July 26, 2004. www.tcm.com/tcmdb/title/129/doctor-zhivago#articles-reviews?articleId=71627.

Miller, Frank. "The Essentials—Random Harvest." Turner Classic Movies, April 30, 2009. www.tcm.com/tcmdb/title/2716/random-harvest#articles-reviews?articleId=71664.

Miller, Frank. Pop Culture 101—Random Harvest." Turner Classic Movies, May 18, 2004. www.tcm.com/tcmdb/title/2716/random-harvest#articles-reviews?articleId=71668.

Miller, John M. "Behind the Camera—A Place in the Sun." Turner Classic Movies, November 9, 2010. www.tcm.com/tcmdb/title/4789/a-place-in-the-sun#articles-reviews?articleId=357292.

Miller, John M. "The Big Idea—A Place in the Sun." Turner Classic Movies, November 9, 2010. www.tcm.com/tcmdb/title/4789/a-place-in-the-sun#articles-reviews?articleId=357291.

Miller, John M. "Dragonwyck." Turner Classic Movies, August 13, 2009. www.tcm.com/tcmdb/title/73599/dragonwyck#articles-reviews?articleId=253031.

Miller, John, and Margarita Landazuri. "A Place in the Sun: The Essentials." Turner Classic Movies, March 21, 2006, www.tcm.com/tcmdb/title/4789/a-place-in-the-sun#articles-reviews?articleId=122454.

Minghella, Anthony, dir. *The English Patient.* Miramax, 1996.

Mitchell, Margaret. *Gone with the Wind.* Pan Books, 1936.

Murray, Rebecca. "Interview with 'Twilight' Author Stephenie Meyer." About.com, movies.about.com/od/twilight/a/stephenie-meyer.htm.

Nashawaty, Chris. "Damon on Fame, Fatherhood, 'Bourne.'" *Entertainment Weekly*, August 6, 2007. www.ew.com/article/2007/08/06/damon-fame-fatherhood-bourne/.

Nathan, Robert. *The Bishop's Wife.* Jeffrey Byron, 2012.

Neuhaus, Mel. "Anna Karenina (1935)." Turner Classic Movies, September 9, 2002. www.tcm.com/this-month/article/532.

Neuhaus, Mel. "The Bishop's Wife." Turner Classic Movies, February 27, 2003. www.tcm.com/tcmdb/title/68818/the-bishops-wife#articles-reviews?articleId=21426.

Nichols, Mike, dir. *The Graduate.* Embassy Pictures, 1967.

Nixon, Rob. "The Big Idea." Turner Classic Movies, March 2, 2007. www.tcm.com/tcmdb/title/2153/pride-and-prejudice#articles-reviews?articleId=158079.

Nixon, Rob. "The Essentials—The Graduate." Turner Classic Movies, January 21, 2010. www.tcm.com/tcmdb/title/18530/the-graduate#articles-reviews?articleId=288405.

Nixon, Rob. "Maurice." Turner Classic Movies, June 2, 2011. www.tcm.com/tcmdb/title/83109/maurice#articles-reviews?articleId=412877.

Nixon, Rob. "My Cousin Rachel." Turner Classic Movies, June 13, 2016. www.tcm.com/tcmdb/title/84298/my-cousin-rachel#articles-reviews.

Nixon, Rob. "Pop Culture 101: Pride and Prejudice." Turner Classic Movies, March 2, 2007. www.tcm.com/tcmdb/title/2153/pride-and-prejudice#articles-reviews?articleId=158085.

Nixon, Rob. "Trivia and Fun Facts About The Graduate." Turner Classic Movies, January 21, 2010. www.tcm.com/tcmdb/title/18530/the-graduate#articles-reviews?articleId=288410.

Nixon, Rob. "Trivia & Fun Facts About Pride and Prejudice." Turner Classic Movies, March 2, 2007. www.tcm.com/tcmdb/title/2153/pride-and-prejudice#articles-reviews?articleId=158086.

Ondaatje, Michael. *The English Patient.* Bloomsbury, 2018.

Pappademas, Alex, host. "We Need More Jet Skis." *The Big Hit Show.* Episode 2. May 11, 2022.

Park, Jennie E. "Carol: 'Less Is More' When Adapting Highsmith." *Creative Screenwriting*, December 2, 2015. www.creativescreenwriting.com/carol-less-is-more-when-adapting-highsmith/.

Passafiume, Andrea. "Behind the Camera—Camille." Turner Classic Movies, December 30, 2011. www.tcm.com/tcmdb/title/1986/camille#articles-reviews?articleId=467327.

Passafiume, Andrea. "The Big Idea—Breakfast at Tiffany's." Turner Classic Movies, February 15, 2007. www.tcm.com/tcmdb/title/21936/breakfast-at-tiffanys#articles-reviews?articleId=156634.

Passafiume, Andrea. "The Big Idea—Camille." Turner Classic Movies, December 30, 2011. www.tcm.com/tcmdb/title/1986/camille#articles-reviews?articleId=467326.

Passafiume, Andrea. "The Big Idea—Laura." Turner Classic Movies, February 27, 2014. www.tcm.com/tcmdb/title/81004/laura#articles-reviews?articleId=961411.

Passafiume, Andrea. "The Bridges of Madison County." Turner Classic Movies, January 28, 2004. www.tcm.com/tcmdb/title/69694/the-bridges-of-madison-county#articles-reviews?articleId=66908.

Pasternak, Boris. *Doctor Zhivago.* Vintage, 2011.

Pasternak Slater, Ann. "Rereading: Doctor Zhivago." *The Guardian*, November 5, 2010. www.theguardian.com/books/2010/nov/06/doctor-zhivago-boris-pasternak-translation.

Polanski, Roman, dir. *Tess.* Columbia Pictures, 1979.

Pollack, Sydney, dir. *Out of Africa.* Universal Pictures, 1985.

Preminger, Otto, dir. *Laura.* Twentieth Century Fox, 1944.

"The Problematic Depiction of False Accusations in Atonement." *Literary Hub*, July 5, 2023.

Proulx, Annie. *Brokeback Mountain.* Scribner, 2005.

Pulver, Andrew. "Girl, Interrupted." *The Guardian*, March 25, 2005. www.theguardian.com/books/2005/mar/26/featuresreviews.guardianreview13.

Quin, Eleanor. "Somewhere in Time." Turner Classic Movies, January 21, 2003. www.tcm.com/tcmdb/title/16578/somewhere-in-time#articles-reviews?articleId=18749.

Reisz, Karel, dir. *The French Lieutenant's Woman*. United Artists, 1981.

Rich, Frank. "Loving Carol." *Vulture*, November 18, 2015. www.vulture.com/2015/11/frank-rich-carol-invisibility-of-lesbian-culture.html.

"A Room with a View." Merchant Ivory. www.merchantivory.com/film/aroomwithaview.

Russell, Ken, dir. *Women in Love*. United Artists, 1969.

Schenkar, Joan. *The Talented Miss Highsmith: The Secret Life and Serious Art of Patricia Highsmith*. St. Martin's, 2010.

Segal, Erich. *Love Story*. Harper Perennial Modern Classics, 2020.

Seton, Anya. *Dragonwyck*. Mariner Books, 1944.

Sharf, Zack. "Britney Spears Gets Teary-Eyed and Runs Lines with Ryan Gosling in 'Notebook' Audition Tape; Casting Director Shares Video and Calls Her 'Phenomenal.'" *Variety*, October 23, 2023. www.variety.com/2023/film/news/britney-spears-the-notebook-audition-ryan-gosling-1235764935/.

Soderbergh, Steven, dir. *Out of Sight*. Universal Pictures, 1998.

Sparks, Nicholas. *The Notebook*. Grand Central, 1996.

Steffen, James. "The Sheik (1921)." Turner Classic Movies, April 7, 2011. www.tcm.com/tcmdb/title/500793/the-sheik#articles-reviews?articleId=387079.

"Steven Soderbergh Interview." *Mr. Showbiz*, 1998.

Stevens, George, dir. *A Place in the Sun*. Paramount Pictures, 1951.

Stevenson, Robert, dir. *Jane Eyre*. Twentieth Century Fox, 1943.

"The Story Behind Twilight." StephenieMeyer.com. Retrieved January 15, 2011.

Sullivan, Kevin Rodney, dir. *How Stella Got Her Groove Back*. Twentieth Century Fox, 1998.

Szwarc, Jeannot, dir. *Somewhere in Time*. Universal Pictures, 1980.

Talbot, Margaret. "Forbidden Love." *New Yorker*, November 22, 2015. www.newyorker.com/magazine/2015/11/30/forbidden-love.

Teo, Hsu-Ming. "Historicizing the Sheik: Comparisons of the British Novel and the American Film." *Journal of Popular Romance Studies* 1, no. 1 (August 4, 2010).

Thompson, Anne. "The Making of 'The Bridges of Madison County.'" *Entertainment Weekly*, June 16, 1995. www.ew.com/article/1995/06/16/making-bridges-madison-county/.

Thompson, Anne. "Todd Haynes and Oscar-Nominated Writer Phyllis Nagy Talk 'Carol,' Glamorous Stars, Highsmith and More." *IndieWire*, January 15, 2016. www.indiewire.com/features/general/todd-haynes-and-oscar-nominated-writer-phyllis-nagy-talk-carol-glamorous-stars-highsmith-and-more-175265/.

Tolstoy, Leo. *Anna Karenina*. Pearson Education, 2008.

Tomalin, Claire. "Love Story: Maurice." Film Review. *Sight & Sound*, Autumn 1987.

Turek, Ryan. "Exclusive Interview: Twilight's Melissa Rosenberg." ComingSoon, August 19, 2008. www.comingsoon.net/horror/news/710594-exclusive-interview-twilights-melissa-rosenberg.

Uprising Creative. "Nicholas Sparks." www.nicholassparks.com/about/.

Valiunas, Algis. "The Man Who Dared." *Commentary*, November 2014. www.commentary.org/articles/algis-valiunas/the-man-who-dared/.

Variety Staff. "Sheridan May Open Sparks' 'Notebook.'" *Variety*, March 10, 1999. www.variety.com/1999/voices/columns/sheridan-may-open-sparks-notebook-1117492169/.

Vidor, Charles, dir. *A Farewell to Arms*. Selznick International Pictures, 1957.

Vieira, Mark A. *Irving Thalberg: Boy Wonder to Producer Prince*. University of California Press, 2009.

Villard, Henry Serrano, and James Nagel. *Hemingway in Love and War: The Lost Diary of Agnes von Kurowsky: Her Letters, and Correspondence of Ernest Hemingway*. Northeastern University Press, 1989.

Walker, Michael R. "A Teenage Tale with Bite." *Brigham Young University Magazine*, Winter 2007.

Waller, Robert James. *The Bridges of Madison County*. Grand Central, 2014.

Webb, Charles. *The Graduate*. Penguin, 2010.

Whitaker, Forest, dir. *Waiting to Exhale*. Twentieth Century Fox, 1995.

White, Lionel. *Obsession*. Stark House, 2024.

Wills, David, ed. *Jean-Luc Godard's "Pierrot Le Fou."* Cambridge University Press, 2000.

Wood, Bret. *Orson Welles*. Greenwood, February 20, 1990.

Wood, Michael. "Before They Met." *London Review of Books*, February 17, 2011. www.lrb.co.uk/the-paper/v33/n04/michael-wood/before-they-met.

Wright, Joe, dir. *Atonement*. Universal Pictures, 2007.

Zackarek, Stephanie. "Jane Eyre (1944)." Turner Classic Movies, November 29, 2011. www.tcm.com/tcmdb/title/79673/jane-eyre#articles-reviews?articleId=461434.

Zamora, Lois Parkinson, and Wendy B. Faris, eds. *Magical Realism*. Duke University Press, 1995.

KRISTEN LOPEZ is an author, entertainment journalist, and disability expert. She has worked as an entertainment journalist for over 15 years, with her articles appearing at *Variety*, MTV, TCM, and Roger Ebert. A California native, Kristen was raised in a small suburb near Sacramento and graduated with a Masters in English from California State University, Sacramento. She is the creator of the classic film podcast, *Ticklish Business*. Based in Los Angeles, she enjoys reading and finding Old Hollywood connections in her neighborhood in her free time. She is the author of *But Have You Read the Book?* and *Popcorn Disability*.

TCM TURNER CLASSIC MOVIES

TURNER CLASSIC MOVIES is the definitive resource for the greatest movies of all time. We entertain and enlighten to show how the entire spectrum of classic movies, movie history, and movie-making touches us all and influences how we think and live today.